BETWEEN
GARDENS

BETWEEN

GARDENS

Observations on Gardening, Friendship and Disability

Carol Graham Chudley
& Dorothy Field

POLESTAR BOOK PUBLISHERS

Polestar Book Publishers acknowledges the ongoing financial support of The Canada Council; the British Columbia Ministry of Small Business, Tourism and Culture through the BC Arts Council; and the Government of Canada through the Book Publishing Industry Development Program (BPIDP).

Edited by Barbara Kuhne
Design by Val Speidel
Cover and interior images: see credits on pages 236–37
Printed and bound in Canada

CANADIAN CATALOGUING IN PUBLICATION DATA

Chudley, Carol Graham, 1938–1998
Between gardens

ISBN 1-896095-55-0
1. Chudley, Carol Graham, 1938–1998 – Correspondence. 2. Field, Dorothy, 1944– – Correspondence. 3. Gardening. 4. Chronic Fatigue Syndrome – Patients – Correspondence. I. Field, Dorothy, 1944– II. Title.
SB450.97.C58 1999635C99-910216-8

LIBRARY OF CONGRESS CATALOGUE NUMBER: 99-61830

Polestar Book Publishers
PO BOX 5238, Station B
Victoria, British Columbia
Canada
V8R 6N4
http://mypage.direct.ca/p/polestar/

In the United States:
Polestar Book Publishers
PO BOX 468
Custer, WA
USA
98240-0468

5 4 3 2 1

Canadä

To Ron and Rudy

PREFACE

I FIRST MET Carol more than twenty-five years ago. We were both artists and craftspeople in a small Vancouver Island community. She was teaching pottery and selling pots; I was a weaver (I later switched to working with handmade paper). We taught at the same community college and I'd exchange milk and eggs from our farm for her pots.

Carol was something of a legend in local circles. For years, she supported herself and her family by selling her work. People came to her studio not just to buy pots but for the pleasure of walking through her wonderland gardens, where plants like spiked teasel and towering cow parsley – plants that no one else paid attention to – grew in a wild gnome's paradise. Carol had a vision for her land, which was an odd acreage that other people had passed by as hopeless. She transformed several plots into linked gardens, tying the wild plants to the cultivated ones. And she was a determined creator, working through problems with her pots or her garden, experimenting with often-radical approaches until she got things to work as she wanted them to.

When Carol bought property down the road from me in 1988, our strong but sporadic friendship settled into a more regular routine. I watched in awe as she turned her weird-shaped swampland into a homestead. By that time, Carol had been suffering from Chronic Fatigue Syndrome (CFS) for about ten years. She had had to give up pottery and could only garden in small chunks of time and with lots of help from her husband Ron, who came into her life just around the time she moved to the new property.

Carol and I shared an interest in gardening, though our approaches and styles were very different. She worked from a more realized vision of the landscape. I tended to be less visionary, gardening in response to the nudging of our farm. When Rudy and I first moved to this land, the "bones" of the place were good – an old house with a few fruit trees and a raspberry patch to get us going – but the farmyard was a bare expanse of wild grass that browned off every summer. Now, twenty-five years later, every corner supports an experiment in fruits, vegetables or old roses. The place is always green and I sometimes think about hacking back this fruiting jungle to create a few hot spots in which to sit and soak up the sun.

This book began in 1995, seven years after Carol and I had become neighbours. I had just returned from a third extended trip to Asia with my family when Carol proposed that we exchange letters about our gardens. She had an idea for a gardening book that she wanted to write and thought the letters might help focus her attention. The idea seemed quirky at first – who writes long letters to a neighbour one sees or speaks to several times a week? – until we actually began corresponding. Then the letters opened up a space in which to delve into thoughts, memories, observations – things there was little space for in the rest of our lives. Since we were in constant contact, there was no need to fill the letters with our daily frustrations or reports on her illness. Instead the correspondence became a forum for a rarer exchange: musings on how to live. Soon Carol's original idea of writing a practical book of garden tips faded. Her time reading and watching TV with a critical eye, and her forays with Ron into the outside world, were fed into her letters as a way to understand and funnel her creative energy. My morning walks and time digging vegetables became compost to share in my letters.

Carol struggled with CFS in an extreme form that included severe back problems as well as hypersensitivity to a list of things too long to name. This sensitivity made it almost impossible to medicate her pain, which increased over time. Minuscule dosages caused extreme side effects. A drug that had worked for days or weeks would suddenly stop working or affect her body in intolerable ways. Any kind of stress – things unpleasant or overly pleasant – exhausted her and put her out of commission for days afterward. During her last years, a mysterious heat and pain appeared, first in her feet, later in her hands and even her face, causing her extremities to swell and peel. Walking, even onto the porch to overlook the garden, became impossible. The pain in her hands made typing unbearable, cutting Carol off from her extensive e-mail network.

Carol's illness was a tourniquet, gradually cutting off her lifeline. In itself it wasn't fatal, and yet it was killing her. She was extraordinarily lucky to have Ron, who devoted himself to caring for her. Cuts to the medical system, on the other hand, made it harder and harder for Carol to get in-home nursing care. The system seemed to view her as a malingerer, as if she had chosen to spend years with ever-shrinking physical capacities.

This book is primarily a collection of letters of friendship and sharing, with the garden as fulcrum – a rare form in this sped-up world. But alongside our correspondence, which bears witness to the oneness

Carol felt with the earth, she also wrote prolifically about her day-to-day anguish over the progress of her illness. Short excerpts of Carol's journal writing are interspersed with our garden letters, a small window into an illness that is so little understood.

꙰

On May 24, 1998, I was woken early to news of a freak accident. Carol had died suddenly before this book was finished. It was a tragic end to years of suffering – as well as a release.

In her struggle to squeeze pleasure from a life wracked with pain, Carol taught me about being alive – how to channel ideas, how to closely watch the quail at the feeder and the dragonflies on the pond, how to savour sweetness in an ever-narrowing world. Carol had enough plans, books to write and illustrate, additions to the garden and ideas for making pots for another fifty jam-packed years. Since her death, when detail and beauty stop me and make me look again, more slowly and with greater attention, I think of her.

I still dream of Carol. She is talking to me, telling stories – one of her great talents. Her voice is animated; images spark. She isn't sick. The publication of this book is bittersweet. It was Carol's main focus in the last months of her life and it seems fair and right to have something tangible, something beautiful, with which to remember her by, she who loved beauty so. And it seems unfair and deeply grievous that Carol is not here to see her vision's fruition.

—DOROTHY FIELD, 1999

CONTENTS

INTRODUCTION

by CAROL GRAHAM CHUDLEY

MY FIRST MEMORY OF Dorothy was when she came into my pottery showroom in the mid-1970s. In her arms was her tiny, crying daughter. I offered to hold Cicely so that Dorothy could enjoy browsing. In the years that followed, our paths crossed in various places: at Malaspina College, where we both taught; at Dorothy's farm, where I bought fresh milk and eggs; at slide shows of the unique world trips she had taken. Each encounter was enjoyable but brief. We were women – like so many others – who tried to do everything. We worked as artists, teachers, mothers and wives, juggling our lives and maintaining a precarious balance, far too busy to stand in one place for very long.

Life changes. Now, our children are grown and gone from home. My life has begun to clear of the chaos wrought by my illness (Chronic Fatigue Syndrome). The time seemed right to start writing to Dorothy in the hope that our letters about gardening experiences would consolidate my idea for a book of gardening tips. Little did I know what would happen. In the year we corresponded, many things became clear to me. I found that I was not interested in writing that gardening book after all. Instead, in one year and forty-two letters I discovered more about myself and found a new way to direct my creative energies. The letters helped knit my life, which had become unraveled by illness, and gave me new focus. I had found a way to encourage and direct a spontaneous out-pouring of interests and feelings.

It has been months since Dorothy left for Asia again, ending our year of letter-writing. I still miss writing to her. I realize, with each passing month, how precious was our year's connection. I crave more of this communication, where each letter is written in solitude, allowing the inner me to speak with clarity. The more time goes by, the more I realize I may never find another person with whom to share in this way.

We all want to be known for the real person we are. Writing a letter to a trusted friend is the closest most of us come to leaving something of ourselves in the hands of another.

I N T R O D U C T I O N

by DOROTHY FIELD

I HAD JUST come back from ten months of travel and research in Asia when Carol asked me if I would be interested in exchanging letters about gardening. I said "sure," not knowing yet what the letters might turn out to be. Though my return from the extended trip was my third, I found myself as unprepared as ever for the confusion of reentry. Everything looked more or less the same, but in truth the ground had shifted in subtle ways during my absence. Friends' lives had changed, political battles were recast. Even the vegetable garden, planted by our tenants and awash in self-sown squash, felt unfamiliar.

In this time of adjustment, the letters became a touchstone — a way to feel my way back onto home ground. There are many forms of meditation and writing letters to Carol became mine. I found myself impatient for Carol's response so that I could legitimately start the next letter. Sometimes I couldn't wait — the ever-shifting images of trees and grass outside my window demanded recording.

As I write these words, I am again just returned from a shorter time in Asia, again trying to find my way home. And the leaves are at it again, registering every possible nuance of scarlet, ochre and grayed green, riding the air currents, sinking on the grass in silent patchwork. Thanks be to leaves, grass, clouds and words like a butterfly net — full of holes, trying to catch the uncatchable.

SUMMER

June 10th *Cool, cloudy beginning (5:30 A.M.,*
52 degrees) 14 pond lilies blooming

Dear Dorothy,

It was so good to see you after almost a year. So much has happened to both of us in that time, yet when we are together again we start talking as if we had never been apart. We touched on many things that are important to me, so I'm excited about continuing our conversation on paper.

You have often quizzed me about my unusual methods of gardening and landscaping. I never thought much about what I was doing all those years: what I did came naturally. With more time and distance and age I have come to believe that I am a gentle caretaker of whatever land on which I live. Lately I have taken great interest in why this could be. One of the dubious perks of my illness and having such a lot of down time is the change from frantic physical activity to lots of thinking. In my healthy years, like most of us, I was caught up in too much action and too little contemplation.

The major life changes from this disease have forced me to assess what direction I should take. I probably never told you this, but I often wrote about nature and gardening during my years of making pottery. I wrote in response to people commenting "Where did you find this plant?" or "What interesting things you do with your garden!" or "I could *never* have a yard like this. I have no green thumb." My writings were meant to be funny and informative, or simply helpful, like the article "Dear Jennifer and Morley," written for the new owners of Briarwood. When they took over my old home I wanted to help them cope with the gardens and know their history.

Over the years I often found myself giving tours of the garden and woods. In the last few years before my illness I took many people on long hikes up behind our property to Rat Lake and beyond. Punctuating our far-ranging conversation would be my running commentary on the flora we were passing. I was surprised that most of my companions didn't know the most common plants and bushes. Even those who hiked regularly or sailed around the islands were not knowledgeable. They were quite interested in what they were seeing, when it was pointed out, and impressed with what I knew. (If you don't know a vanilla leaf or a shepherd's purse, then your tour guide must seem brilliant!) My love of plants led to my nickname, Carol Teaselseed, which I still treasure.

When I was on the committee fighting to prevent the Alpex developers from cutting hundreds of acres of wonderful, wild beauty into small lots, I took neighbours, politicians and lawyers up to that land. Most had never walked those acres, which are less than one-half mile from their homes and the main highway. One walk would galvanize them into converts for preserving that land. I realized that 99 percent of people have no idea of the lay of the land, the value, the beauty and uniqueness of this area. When they actually get off the highway, out of their own apartment or home and out of the designated parks, they are stunned with what is right under their noses.

I decided then that I would like to conduct nature tours. You don't have to make a trip to find nature: just take an hour and some walking shoes and start right here. You don't need to hike the West Coast Trail with heavy backpacks for five days. Anyway, fate intervened and I was unable to realize that plan. The walking is gone, but not my love and excitement about nature.

≈

My first memories of my surroundings and of plants in particular are from the small towns where I spent my childhood. In the 1940s, where I lived, most streets were accompanied by alleys – little travelled, weedy, with garden escapees flourishing in wild abandon, as were we, the children. Those alleys were our playgrounds, and I loved them.

My first flower memories were of tall hollyhocks lining the tracks of the alleys. We made dolls of the flowers and buds, elegant women dressed in long gowns of white, pink and mauve. It was summer play for children left to our own explorations. I am so grateful for those days of freedom. We were unsupervised for hours, days, weeks, it seems. For years our parents instructed us to "Go out and play," and we did. I remember running through glades of lily-of-the-valley, so many you could not help stepping on them. Someone must have planted them at some time, and because the location was perfect for them, they naturalized (went wild). In my fifty years since then I have tried to find a place where lily-of-the-valley would take over and I have not succeeded yet. But this principle is the basis of all my gardening and my so-called "green thumb": find things that grow easily in the places where you garden.

While you have been admiring my style of gardening, I have been watching you and Rudy developing and expanding your farm. Everyone who sees it admires it. How did this come about?

⤜

The morning is getting away and I must get on with this day. First off I have to check the bees at the back. How are they managing with no shelter in this cold, cold rainy snap?

Love, Carol

June 17th

Dear Carol,

I was interested to learn that you have lily-of-the-valley visions from your childhood. I grew up on three acres edged in woods. It had been gardened intensively by the former owners. When I was very young there were large perennial beds laid out on the lawns, but gradually they gave way to grass as my mother realized the limits of her time and patience. Even so, a magic place remained, a shaded hillock of solid lily-of-the-valley stretching up to an outcropping of grey glaciated rock. It didn't require any care, and every spring I revelled in the gratuitous gift of that scent.

Another special place for me was a grove of purple lilacs. I called it the Lilac Inn (after a Nancy Drew mystery), and I would cuddle against the twisty branches, finding shelter from the hot summer sun under the heart-shaped leaves.

There was an enormous transparent apple tree that lit up in early summer. Only one side bloomed each year, but still there were far too many apples to eat. They covered the ground in a bumpy carpet, first yellow-green, then brown and rich-smelling, drawing hordes of wasps. Out from the screened porch were two huge old apple trees, grey, gnarled and bending into each other – the Sad Sisters. They were russets, fall apples, with a tart flavour I loved. We would gather the windfalls in October and drive them off to a cider mill, coming home with gallon jugs of amber juice. We could never drink it all before it turned hard, so the last jugs sat by the kitchen door freezing and thawing until they cracked. Years after I left home one of the Sad Sisters crashed to the ground, was sawn up and carted away. The other one stood alone then, in silent vigil, still bending toward the one no longer there.

Around the periphery of the Sad Sisters were dwarf peach trees, which produced loads of fuzzy thick-skinned peaches. I remember one summer of Gillette commercials touting razor blades "sharp enough to shave the fuzz off a peach." I tried it. The skin broke. Year by year the peach trees died, leaving more and more smooth green space on the lawn.

I can't think of those trees and lawns without thinking of Fanny, a distant cousin about my grandmother's age. She came to live with us when I was three, and she cooked steadily and lovingly: challah, marble cake, schnecken, homemade noodles and of course regular food. I have a vision of her holding a brimming bowl of red sour cherries against her generous breasts. She is wearing a printed apron over a printed housedress. She has just come down the ladder from picking and is standing triumphant in the sun before going back to the kitchen to bake them into cherry turnovers. Sometime after that, lightning struck the cherry tree, splitting it irreparably. I couldn't understand why my parents never replaced the tree.

The mint fared better. I would go with Fanny to the ditch by the derelict vegetable garden where the mint rampaged. We picked great bunches for the gallons of iced tea that was our constant summer drink.

As I write this I understand more clearly the energy source for these last twenty years on this farm, endlessly planting more fruit trees, more berry bushes than we can easily take care of or harvest. That childhood garden was the source of gifts. They came every year, free, freely given.

I remember the raspberry patch. My father had no concept of wiring the canes so they grew in a dense matted mass. I would crawl underneath, pop up like a loon somewhere in their midst and just eat and eat and eat. I don't remember ever picking into a bowl. No one canned or froze them. We didn't prepare for winter; we lived for the moment and then it was gone.

I think of the wild cherry, a spindly sprawling tree up by the road, loaded with tiny sweet cherries. We'd climb the tree, crouch in the branches and eat, like the raccoons on the chicken coop roof on our farm now, spitting the seeds to the ground. The raccoons leave rank piles of black droppings. At least we didn't do that.

As to your question about how things have evolved on this farm, it has all been pretty hit and miss. I've read a bit about landscape architecture and the bones of the garden but mostly I've just stuck things in here and there and hoped they'd grow. Often they didn't. Some failures were drastic enough to warrant more planning and research. My third attempt at an herb garden finally worked. I had never initiated a garden until we rented a small house when we first moved to Canada. Rudy had gardened before and had some basic concepts. I read a Rodale Press pocketbook on organic gardening, then sat in the dirt and cried – it all seemed too hard.

This seems like a fruitful meditation. I am at a time where I need to re-evaluate my relationship to all these trees we've planted. Part of me longs for a small shack overlooking a reedy marsh, where I can watch the blackbirds light on the cattails and never have to think about canning or freezing again. Meanwhile, yesterday I dutifully planted rows and rows of beans, just in case winter comes again.

Love, Dorothy

June 19th   *Another cold morning*   *48 degrees at 6 A.M.*

Dear Dorothy,

I read your letter when I got up from my nap and was very excited by your childhood memories, which are so similar to and yet so different from mine. I tried my best to find an "Aunt Bea" person in my childhood, like your Fanny, but there was none. I realize that I have no memories of eating food of any kind from gardens during my childhood. Certainly no one cooked well. In fact the family stories are usually about how bad a cook Granny was, or how awful Aunt Dolly's cakes were.

Our little family moved seven times from the time I was born until I was twelve, and there were no old, established gardens in my childhood. What I remember, though, was being in the woods all the time on the outskirts of the small towns where we lived.

I love your Sad Sisters image. The first nature spot that I named was Moss Hill. I remember once going to a girl scouts meeting and learning how to make a cooker out of a big tin can by cutting a smoke hole at the top and a fire feeder hole at the bottom. I was so thrilled with this that I took a friend to my favourite place, Moss Hill. (This was in Illinois, so I think it was more likely a moss mound.) I cooked bacon on top of this can and made bacon sandwiches that tasted so good. I never went back to girl scouts, though, probably because of the uniform.

⬿

The first time I got a clear picture of how a garden could be was when I moved to Canada. I visited a new friend who was living in a rental house in Duncan here on Vancouver Island. The whole backyard was a jungle. Except for paths, it was a solid tangled growth of raspberries. Originally someone probably planted neat rows and tied them up, but through a series of renters, the raspberries had their way. Without any watering, fertilizing or pruning, they provided enough raspberries for about half the town. We walked around picking, and I thought, "Gracious this is easy." They seemed to grow about as easily as our own wild black-berries do.

I remember another vivid gardening experience when I visited an aunt and uncle who lived on ten acres in Oregon. They had hauled out all the old refuse from a graveyard for old cars and discovered a wonderful pond, complete with a little rowboat. Growing there at the water's edge, with roots in the muck, was a twosome: a tree with a grapevine twisting round it. High in the air were the grapes. My aunt harvested more grapes than she could use from that one vine, which grew untended for years in a wet area, using a living tree for a trellis. They never pruned it or watered it or fertilized it. Triumph over adversity. Great huge delicious purple grapes for the taking.

～

No matter how I try to remember, I have no childhood recollection of seeing anyone planting a vegetable garden or canning produce. In fact I have a morbid fear of canned goods on account of my mother's oft-re-peated story of a small town in Kansas that was wiped out by botulism from home-canned goods at a community picnic.

The first garden I planted was when I was in the third grade, in Centralia, Illinois. I was eight years old. I have a very vivid image of digging a plot of earth at the back of the large lot, near a shed and an alley. It was 1947 – the polio years – and down the street was a large institutional hospital, The Sister Kenney Foundation. Since neither of my parents ever prepared a garden, I must have seen someone else doing it. Anyway, I seemed to know to turn over the earth to get it ready, and I remember shovelling over and over, in anticipation of spring coming.

My first plants were rare specimens that I found along the alley – where else? I now know that they were plantains. I especially prized the ones with thick mottled leaves that were variations on the usual green. I transplanted these wild things into rows in my plot. I haven't tried trans-planting plantain since (why would I?), but think they would be difficult. Apparently then they were not, as I have memories of rows of beautiful plants.

This scene in my mind is as if viewed through a hazy, foggy window, replaying itself endlessly. I remember the feel of the soil as it crumbled

in my fingers. Many, many seasons of crumbling earth and wonderful tactile sensations have transpired between that first garden and now. Sometimes I wonder, "Did it happen?"

I am so grateful that no one told me how to garden. No one gave me seeds to plant or a "starter kit." No one stood over my shoulder or denigrated my unusual interests. I was allowed to transplant weeds, admiring the mutants, having no opinions about their worth, seeing them with innocent, adoring eyes. No one gave me rules. I did not lack ideas or enthusiasm for exploring. The funny thing is that if I saw a child as inquisitive and self-motivated as I was, I would feel compelled to "enrich" her environment. Something to think about, huh?

Another cloudy, cool day coming up. The bees are doing fine. They are leaving more of their combs exposed. Our "back 40" now has permanent paths from our frequent trips to "check the bees," as if we are minding them – as if we can do anything for them. The combs are so beautiful, so perfect, like off-white saucers hanging in order. Seen from the west side, when the early morning sun illuminates them from behind, they are like porcelain, edges translucent and fragile.

Love, Carol

CAROL'S JOURNAL

A whole lot of things have been brewing inside me since I heard the latest news flash about "neurally mediated hypotension." If this has been a part of my illness from the beginning, I feel robbed. I have been showing all the symptoms but no doctor ever really listened or took the time to investigate. Seven years ago I went to a neurologist and explained all my symptoms, including the strange "inability to stand in one place," how ill I felt when forced into a standing position. He replied, "I think you should think of the psychological reasons why you don't like to stand." I explained that I could not stand up even to have a conversation or watch a bird or prune a tree. No matter what the activity, I had to sit down. He didn't pursue any diagnosis.

I have just spent ten years in limbo, with hell-on-wheels for a physical life and fatigue beyond belief. I feel as though on a roller coaster of emotions. I can hardly allow myself to think that I might get better ... It's scary to think I might get my energy back, that I might walk up Cobble Hill Mountain again, that I might be able to run and garden and talk to people. This fear must be like when an inmate has been locked up for years and is about to be let out into the real world. But of course my real fear is that the treatment won't work and that I will be left here living in limbo.

On CNN Medical News the other day two doctors were talking about CFS and exercise. One doctor encourages as much exercise as the patient can do. The other one showed "proof" that brain damage occurs (he believes irreversible) when a patient "pushes." It's so hard to know how much to do. You can get a setback of days, weeks or months from overdoing it. Even these researcher-doctors don't understand why CFS patients' bodies get so out of shape.

After these many years of illness, I'm finally accepting myself with lots of "limitations." I've learned a new lifestyle that includes quiet activities, naps, bird watching, enjoying smaller things. If a person had known me before, it would look like a complete turnaround.

June 22nd

Dear Carol,

Your story of the grape growing up the tree reminded me again of the house where I grew up. Just at the edge of the woods was a rose that rambled into a dogwood tree. No one helped it; no one tried to get in its way. It was the kind of thing you would never notice except during the few short weeks when the tree was trimmed in pale pink blooms. I loved that wildness. It reminds me of another sight – bright clumps of daffodils growing at an abandoned whaling station on the Queen Charlotte Islands. I was touched by their tenacity, the poignancy of their persistence, when the only sign of those who planted them was an empty cellar hole. Below my family's dogwood were bushes we called mountain laurel, which had clusters of pink blossoms crimped like tiny cups for a fairy tea party. No scent that I can recall, but I remember their delicate form and the distinct tiny stamens in their open centres.

These memories interest me. For years my mother tended a perennial border. I remember her pleasure when she felt it was working, though I have no recollection of how it looked. My memories are of the fruit trees and the shadowy woods full of jack-in-the-pulpits and Dutchmen's breeches. I used to fiddle with plants: splitting plantain leaves along their veins, using my fingernails to sculpt designs in russet apples and squeezing the red fleshy parts of yew seeds.

One of my favourite gardens is in Idaho where some friends went "back to the land" many years ago. They lived in a yurt surrounded by lush circular beds of gargantuan herbs gone wild – drifts of starry white valerian, towering spikes and leaves of elecampane. Their outhouse bobs up in a sea of pinky purple opium poppies. There is an extravagant feel to this garden, set amidst scrubby pines.

This is how I most like to garden – as a matchmaker who introduces a modest flower to a shy spot of land and watches them hit it off so well that I am irrelevant. It is part of my natural laziness. Years ago I planted a violet-blue clematis in front of a weathered wooden fence. Things went badly and the clematis got smaller instead of bigger, then disappeared. I forgot about it until early one summer many years later I noticed large blue flowers nestled between the red leaves of a Japanese plum. It took a while to remember that I'd planted that vine, which grows happier now that its top has stretched to the sun.

I was very impressed with your story of your early gardening efforts. I was never so self-directed. One summer my mother decided my younger brother and I should have a garden of our own, but I don't remember anything in it except nasturtiums. They grew like crazy and I loved their violent orange colour. Later I planted nasturtiums between my squash plants – as suggested in a companion gardening book – and they went absolutely crazy, returning year after year. We ate the flowers and the leaves and I pickled the seeds into what are optimistically called "capers." I love to come into the garden just before dark when everything goes grey and muted except those siren nasturtiums. Now they have gone so wild that they strangle the beans, and I force myself to pull them out. But I always leave too many, forgetting how big they get, so the struggle goes on throughout the summer.

The other day Rudy was tying a grape along its wires when he noticed that a sprawling rose that grows on the opposite wall had stretched a long cane across the wires and was now growing out to meet the grape-vine. He asked me what he should do. I knew he wanted permission to train the rose back into its allotted area. I was thrilled to see it growing out of bounds, making a kind of poetry on the wires. Still, there comes a time when I let things get so out of hand that I need someone with a firmer sense of discipline. Something about balance, I guess.

From my window I can see an Oriental poppy blooming up between some flagstones I placed last summer. I invited nothing there except some creeping thyme. Now the poppy is there, a blood orange colour, deeper than the nasturtiums, and it emerges just where my chair should be. I am conflicted about its presence – torn between delight in its unex-pected appearance and annoyance that it is in the wrong spot. So it goes.

The jasmine is taking over this whole side of the house. Tomorrow I will have to hack it back before it blocks out all the light from these windows.

Love to you, Dorothy

June 26th   *10 water lilies bloomed yesterday.*
Summer has come!

Dear Dorothy,

I guess Rudy told you that I stopped by your garden to see the rose reaching to the grapes and the poppy growing where it shouldn't. It made me think of you and Rudy and how gardening with a partner is a revealing experience. I could write a volume about that.

It's easy to look at people's yards and gardens and never fathom how they got the way they are. The gardeners influence every tree, bush, vine, flower, vegetable and blade of grass. Think of the discussion, the thought that went into each plant, and the love that is invested. When it looks so easy, as your yard does, I can understand why people are overwhelmed by a garden and think that some magic happens.

≈

A wonderful thing happened to me when I was in fourth grade: I got my first pair of glasses. I remember walking to school that first day and seeing things that were awesome: individual leaves on the trees, and my friends' faces. Before that, my world was like an underwater blur. Years later when I discovered impressionist painters, I wondered if they were nearsighted! I believe my early nearsighted view of the world influences what I consider natural, beautiful and correct. Even now I love to take off my glasses and look at the whole other beautiful world that is there. A strange phenomenon occurs when I'm without glasses: I feel almost invisible. If I can't see you, you can't see me. I find this a great help when I have to eat alone in public.

I love all variations of green, lots of green with small amounts of other colour interspersed, much as you find in nature. My favourite is "spring green," what Robert Frost called "gold":

> Nature's first green is gold,
> Her hardest hue to hold.

I can get lost in looking at greens. Ron and I joke that my world is a "green painting" and what I love is getting it just right. I sit in my lounge chair looking down the orchard, revelling in the greens of the apple trees, the Leylandi hedge, the wisteria, honeysuckle, grapevines, lilacs, irises and hydrangeas. Beyond are the bits of colour from "Ron's Rock Garden" peeking through the greens: yellow, orange and pink poppies, purple veronica, and yellow-and-white "no names." Now the apples are beginning to make themselves evident, spots of yet another green. The canvas is complete with the backdrop of dark evergreens and the various grasses growing in between.

At the end of the planting season I always take my leftover flower seedlings and plant them all over the yard, wherever they can be safe from the lawnmower. These small bright surprises finish the painting, as do the many plants I bring in from the roadsides (trifids, martians, etc.). And last but not least the native plants add their own spots of colour: blackberry blooms, ocean spray, St. John's Wort, dandelions, daisies, buttercup and even thistle, until Ron finds them.

When I first came to this area of Canada, people would ask, "Don't you miss the spectacular fall colours of the East?" As a matter of fact I don't. I love our fall colours because they are always interspersed with the dark greens of the fir, pine, hemlock and cedar. Fall colours tastefully sprinkled in my green painting. When the colours are finished, I know the evergreen needles will still be there, along with the evergreen broadleaf trees and bushes and the mosses and ferns. Always a living green painting available for my enjoyment.

Did I tell you about the autobiography of an autistic woman, *Nobody Nowhere*? I enjoyed Donna Williams' description of grass — obviously a very different "seeing," but one I could relate to. We "normal" people think that we all see pretty much alike, but I *know* that we do not.

An orb web spider has set up camp stretched between two of the bookcases. We have to remember not to reach into that area. Most of the time he is not visible. Right now the first sunlight is hitting his web. It is gold and he is busy repairing his trap.

I want to get outside to explore the yard and see what has changed since last night. Yesterday the purple water iris bloomed, the first bloom of the season. And of course I have to check the bees.

Love, Carol

July 1st

Dear Carol,

I thought of Robert Frost's gold this morning when I was taking my walk. The wild grasses along the road have come into flower. My favourites are the silky fine ones. In the early morning sun they are golden, lit like networks of spun silk, so elegant in their absolute commonness there along the verges of the road.

The road edges have been my inspiration over these last six years of walking through cold clear mornings, grey drippy mornings and this brief hot time. They keep me grounded, show me exactly where we are in the season. Right now the wild chicory is in bloom. The plants are dishevelled, asymmetric and awkward, but the flowers are astral-blue daisies with fine white tongues in their centres. The vetch is out as well, a slightly more lavender blue, and along one stretch I saw a patch of butter-and-eggs, one of my childhood favourites.

I remember when I first found the wild orchids along the road, calypsos, coralroot, and rattlesnake plantain. They grow in our woods but there they seem protected. Along the road's edge they seem so vulnerable, I experienced a gut fear for them. No one notices them, though, unless they are walking, and the walkers I pass are all too gentle to harm them. So they persist, coming back each spring.

There is so much beauty along the roadsides: tiny spherical elderberries, bright red on their purple stems; lush white salmonberry flowers metamorphosing into translucent orange berries; pale pink twin flowers, born like tiny trumpets on their forked stalks. But I also admire plants that are not considered beautiful: the burdock stalks as they ripen their rusty seeds; the tiny yellow senecio flowers, so frail and disorganized, which shine like stars under the dark shadowing firs; and the frenetic calligraphy of the dried black seed pods on the sprawling vetch vines. I pull burdock ruthlessly when it shows up in the grass around the house – it spreads like wildfire and has taproots that grow straight to hell. Along the road, though, I can wonder at the architecture of its seeds, like tiny ribbed space capsules, with no thought of trying to discipline it. It's just another part of the way things are – wild, mysterious and beyond my control.

Since my last letter I have been thinking about why I plant what I plant. It has more to do with memories and associations than with any sensible garden plan. Three lilacs were here when we bought the farm, but I have planted a few more. I needed them for their memories of the "Lilac Inn" and because they signify places lived in over long years. Across the Prairies I kept seeing them marking old doorways. Around here they grow into huge spreading groves.

We built the arbour over the stone terrace mostly so that I could plant wisteria on the cedar supports. There was wisteria all across the front of the house where I grew up and the neighbours down the road had an outdoor room roofed with clouds of trailing blue wisteria.

I have Oriental poppies because of those Monet scenes of green hillsides dotted with orangey-red blooms. I have red currants in memory of the red ones and the white ones that I loved to strip and eat when I was a kid. Somehow their taste now is not as intoxicating as it was then, but I still remember the feeling of loss when we had to pull them out because they were host to a pest that threatened the red pines.

Sometimes I plant trees for people: a hazelnut when Cicely was born, a Korean dogwood when Rudy's mother died. Other plants remind me of the people who gave them to me: the translucent yellow peony from Peg, first of the perennials to bloom in the spring; the wild cyclamen from old Bea Palmer who had woods full of wildflowers she transplanted; the now-huge wild cherry tree that started life as a sucker in another friend's garden.

I plant many things for their smell: jasmine, witch hazel, February daphne and, of course, the old roses. At this season the jasmine perfumes the air in our bedroom and the bathroom. It's so strong, it's almost cloying.

Planting is the easy part, especially since Rudy does most of the endless watering during the hot dry summer spells. It is keeping up with their demands that weighs on me. I seem to get lazier each year, but that doesn't stop me from hatching new schemes, new ideas of things to plant. More and more, though, I plant some celandine in this corner, move some borage there, knowing that with luck they'll take off

and spread and there won't really be anything for me to do except be glad.

How are the bees? Our hay is down and if we're lucky it will get baled this afternoon. I hope so. It only got rained on once, very lightly. Most years it gets rained on several times and gradually turns a dead dun colour before it's baled.

Love to you, Dorothy

CAROL'S JOURNAL

First thing in the morning I go on my walk and I am full of plans and bright ideas for whatever we are working on, and then by 11 a.m. I cannot put together a full sentence and am unable to remember how I could have thought I could do all that. After a nap and the return of some subdued energy, I am again flabbergasted that I could be so forgetful of reality that I made all those plans. Chronic Fatigue Syndrome is sort of like a daily manic-depressive disease, except that I am neither manic nor depressive. I guess it's more like an exuberant-fatigued disease. No one but Ron sees this transformation. It is as predictable as the clock, and very unrelenting. Even when I have "better days," the up and down cycle is predictable. I have about two hours of fairly OK energy and muscle in the afternoon. If I use it up, I have to stop everything. If I can take it very, very slowly I can last until 4 p.m. or a bit later.

Yesterday Ron and I had to go to Duncan to the insurance place, but by 4:15 I had already gone into fatigue mode. So we put me in the tub, lying down in warm water, and I stayed there for about ten minutes. Lying in the warm tub encourages blood to flow to my brain, allowing me a bit more energy — sort of like squeezing the last bit of toothpaste out of a tube. We usually make appointments for when I can handle it, so don't often have to do this, but there are times when we cannot bend the world to me.

Ron helped me to get up from the tub and get dressed and into the car. I had to use the lying down seat, and when we got to the insurance place I stayed outside while Ron did all the paperwork and then got me to come in just for signing. Immediately after we went home and I lay down on the couch. The whole thing shows how I really cannot function according to "world time."

July 3rd 7 *water lilies blooming. Cool and overcast!*

Dear Dorothy,

I have been thinking about our phone conversation last night and wishing that I had taped it. It was so full of things that are important. Every once in a while I pause in my channel surfing and catch part of a gardening show. There are so many of them, just as there are mountains of gardening books on the shelves at Volume I Bookstore. They are beautiful and slick, lush yet sterile, like paint-by-number kits. I vividly remember doing paint-by-numbers when I was very young. Now I cannot help wondering, What if I had been given a box of oil paints and blank canvases instead? Do all those TV programs and books on gardening actually teach and inspire, or do they merely entertain and contribute to the cult of perfectionism? Is it like watching sports – does owning the books become a substitute for physical activity? Something to ponder.

When I taught ceramics at Malaspina College, that last year of my teaching career, I felt very inspired. The first class of the semester was three hours long, and I took the students outside to dig some clay. This was easy because clay is not precious; it's everywhere. Thankfully that day we only had to dig about a foot to find some. We took bags of the greyish clay into the classroom and made it wetter and squishy, then made small clay objects: beads, animals, charms. While the students quickly dried their objects over an oven, I started a wood fire outside on the gravel. Then we sat around talking and slowly pushed the clay objects toward the fire and finally into its red-hot centre. By the end of the three-hour class, magic had happened. We pulled out salmon-coloured beads, animals and charms. "This is how to make pottery," I said. "It's this easy. Anything more we learn together during the semester is merely refinement."

Gardening is this way: you don't have to learn anything to garden. Beyond a few obvious things that we all know – dig a hole, drop in a seed or a transplant, water it and let it germinate. Refinements beyond this come quite naturally in their time and with the inclination of the gardener. I'm glad that no one made it harder for me when I was starting out.

Since you and I both agree that the only gardening wisdom we have we learned through experience, we have no garden secrets, as such, to pass on. Each piece of the earth is different and changing, so our experiences are our own. There are only "the basics" to start with. When I first started reading gardening books, there were only a few classics: Ruth Stout, the Nearings, etc. What they had in common, as I recall, was the assurance that their method was correct and/or revolutionary. I think more likely what they did was uniquely tailored for their spot of land and their needs.

When I was an aspiring potter, self-taught for two years and yearning to learn more, an old hand at it told me this: "Go to six teachers, one at a time. Learn and do everything each teacher tells you is the correct way. At the end of the six you will find your own way." I think that about sums up my bit of wisdom on how to use "gardening experts." Reading gardening books helps, but I have found more wisdom from people around me. Every community has wise and knowledgeable people, living ordinary lives, doing extraordinary things, quite unnoticed.

Over the years, when I was busy making pottery, people would walk through my gardens and exclaim about my green thumb. I was too busy to say anything but the simple truth: "It's easy, really: just dig the soil, plant and water." No one believed me because they were looking at gardens I had been working on for seven or eight years, each year learning and adding.

I want to inspire people to see how easy it is. If you write enough about gardening to fill a book, you have written too much. Because to start with you need very little information, you just need confidence. Luckily when I first started gardening, I thought that growing things was easy. And it was.

⪻

As I read your letters, Dorothy, I realize how much alike we are. Like you, I love roadways and railways. I used to walk every day, miles and miles. Now I no longer can do that, but I do the same looking from the van window. With me as his constant teacher, Ron is becoming knowledgeable about the wildflowers. He has become aware of the familiar and recognizes what appears different or odd. When he says excitedly,

"What is that yellow flower?" and I answer, "That is bird's foot trefoil," we both double up in laughter. Has he honestly forgotten the name, or does he just want me to say it again? I am surely a lover of the common names of those seldom-heralded wildflowers of the roadsides and waste-lands.

The combs of the bees are turning from that bone white to a some-what mottled gold and rust – hard to describe. Definitely something is happening in there. The bees are busy making bee magic.

Love, Carol

July 13th
Dear Carol,

I feel that I have to confess: Gardening hasn't always been easy for me, though it's getting easier as I understand better the discrepancy between my grandiose visions and my energy – and as I learn to let the land grow what it loves to grow. Do you know my story about the sweet cicely? It took me ages to find some when I wanted to plant it in honour of our daughter Cicely. It wasn't common around here when she was tiny, but I finally got a plant established in a corner by the herb garden. Then I be-gan to see volunteers popping up everywhere – too many. So one sum-mer I grabbed a handful of ripe seeds and threw them out the back so they wouldn't squeeze out all the other herbs. Next spring I noticed sweet cicely where I'd thrown the seeds. In a few years it was a hedge, a glorious twenty- or thirty-foot hedge along the fence-line that had been ragged and unkempt before. It looked as if someone had designed it that way — some spirit of earth in conjunction with rain and filtered sunlight did it. That's how I'd most like to garden.

But the herb garden was a nightmare. We had an old stone well casing, all grey and lichen-pocked, which I thought would be the perfect centre for an herb garden. Years and years ago I dug in some flagstone to make a circular bed around it and planted a variety of herbs that people gave me. I didn't know about invasiveness — within a short time the oregano began to spread. I was too soft-hearted to take drastic measures, so it overtook everything until I had only oregano. It even squeezed out the pennyroyal. Meanwhile, the grass had grown through, up and over the flagstones so the path was totally obscured. I looked at the mess for years, feeling overwhelmed. One year I dug out the flagstones, then fell into a slough of despond over the pitted earth where the flagstones had been. A summer or two later I marked out two concentric circles, dug down and laid plastic, sand and bricks to make a real path. After that I gave up again, overwhelmed at having to dig out and rework the soil where the oregano grew. Eventually I dug out the dreadful soil left from when they put in the well, and treated myself to a gluttony of new herbs and two old roses. They are still there, mostly flourishing.

That's how I learned about invasion. When I saw how fast the newly planted pennyroyal spread once there was no oregano to kill it off, I dug it out and moved it to a corner. That's my secret now. I plant invasive things judiciously where I'm happy if they go mad. I've got a mound of oregano at the corner of my studio and we get along fine. I'm hoping the borage will grow into clumps around the lilacs and roses, though I hate it in the vegetable garden. The pennyroyal is happy at the base of a wisteria, though the chickens love to scratch away at it, so there's an on-going struggle.

Some things that other people – you, for example – have great luck with, haven't worked here. I tried and tried to get the trifids you gave me to naturalize. No luck at all. I've been coaxing the tansy that spreads so madly in all sorts of places to take over the driveway – in another twenty years it may be bigger than the small clump it now confines itself to. Years ago I had all sorts of California poppies growing in the lawn. I loved them. Then they disappeared. Plants come, they go. There is no accounting. I remember the miracle when I discovered a pine tree growing in the woods in back. We have Douglas fir there, true fir, hemlock and lots of cedar but no pines at all, and none close by that I know of. The one pine seedling is still there, taller than I am now. And there's a dogwood that appeared one year and grew taller and taller, but ever so spindly. Finally when I thought it would never bloom, it did. These are great gifts, these gifts of chance and serendipity.

I have been gardening on this farm for twenty-two years. In the early days I knew almost nothing about plants and not a whole lot about myself. Someone told me growing perennials was easy: You put them in and they come up every year. So I dug a border and then a year or two later enlarged it and sometime after that made it wider. Now it's full of my favourite spring perennials – tree peonies and regular peonies, delphiniums, true lilies and day lilies, irises (not the tall, bearded ones, the medium ones that don't intimidate me). And for about four to six weeks it looks great. That's if I can get it weeded in early spring. Since I first dug it, my back has gotten bad and I have to time myself when weeding. No more

than an hour at a time or I get thoroughly crippled. After the spring flowers, the weeds start up and I lose heart. I'm not good at such maintenance,
especially since there's always too much to do in the vegetable garden
during the summer.

I know that to have gardens look the way they do in gardening books
you have to give them a steady attention, not the fits and starts that are
my wont. Here it is survival of the fittest. If I only plant things I like,
mostly I'm happy with what comes out on top.

I am impatient, too. I can't bear to leave the proper space for trees
and shrubs to grow into, so there are always conflicts after a few years.
But generally I'm happy with the garden these days. After twenty years,
the place begins to have the feeling I wanted it to have — grown over
with vines, a series of open spaces between small trees, with the great
firs in the background. But I love sun, wait all year for these two summer months, and now as the trees begin to fill in, I see it is time to start
carving out some sun spaces again. It's an endless cycle.

When we first moved here there was a natural clearing in the woods,
as if root rot had killed off a large circle of trees. Gradually alders
are beginning to come in and the clearing is getting fuzzier. I like to
watch the succession, seeing what it will do without any interference
from me.

From my window I see bunches of columbine that have gone to seed.
When we first came here there were many; then for some reason they
thinned out, becoming almost sparse. Now I let the seeds ripen, then
scatter them all around, and they are returning to their former splen-
dour. They have cross-pollinated into amazing varieties — all mauvey

pinks and purply blues. Now if only I could convince the foxgloves to move in. They come and then they go. Fickle plants. For some reason they love it just across the fence-line.

The learning for me is about coming into harmony with what I can manage and what I love, giving up visions of magazine gardens for a looser, more eccentric sprawl. I'm trying to live in the garden's moment, being with the apples as they green out, then flush red – then cascade down when the geese shake them out of the bottom branches for easy picking. Being thrilled that the poppyseed poppies have reappeared in the garden after an absence of several years. Recognizing that there are only so many areas a person can be obsessive about, and that the garden doesn't need me for that … Some kind of movement into freedom.

How many water lilies this week?

Love, Dorothy

July 25th   *7 lilies*

Dear Dorothy,

Your letter of July 13th made many things become clearer for me. How could it be that I say gardening is easy while you say gardening has been hard, and yet now we come together and seem to be in the same spot of loving and working in our gardens in a very similar way? We appear, over the years, to have been working from rather opposite ends of the spectrum, and now have come to a very similar place.

My latest venture, a real flower garden, only came last year. Ron cleared a round bed that I used only for annuals: cosmos, geranium,

strawflowers, petunias, nicotiana, pansies, cornflowers and some "no-names." Before that I never had just a flower garden. I was so pleased with it last year: One of my prized photos is of that garden taken through the leaves of the apple trees.

This year that flower garden is already changing. It still has flowers, but purposely I've added two rose bushes and two peonies that will grow huge and take over, along with five purple cabbages, my accidental squash and some volunteer tomatoes. When the tomatoes become too big, they will be turfed out – actually given to a friend who lost all her garden to deer. I plan to eliminate the most "work-intensive" flowers, you see. I love a casual look as well as the casual touch. What appears to be a jumble of beauty is actually guided by me.

The very thing that you love, I have always loved and encouraged: rampant growth of easy plants, so that my only job is to hack out paths through them, seeding casually all the plants I love, many of them the roadside wild things. My favourite spots are the "wastelands." In Victoria I can tell you which vacant lot near Capital Iron has white and buff-coloured chicory, where you can easily find oyster plants (on the hillside where they park the city buses), where every shade of California poppies can be harvested, and which curve along the highway has easy-to-grow bachelor buttons in every colour.

I know many homestead sites and have raided them over the years for lilacs, cornflowers, ivies, various shades of bluebells and ground covers I have no name for. Almost everything in my yard either was here when I came or I brought it here with a long history behind it. Both Ron and I are very aware of how we feel about the yard when young children come and start stepping where they shouldn't. It looks like the wilds to them, but to us it is not.

I can tell you just where you can dig "martians," along which bends in the highway they grow. I monitor their progress each year. Some years they grow like monsters, making me wonder why the six o'clock news has not featured them as some outer space growth. Some years the roads department chops them down before they are four feet tall, and they struggle to grow again, and do. I know all the spots where the teasel grows, including an old milk farm near Fulford Harbour on Saltspring Island. A feeling of warmth comes over me whenever I pass a spot where my plant friends used to grow.

When I think back to my childhood memories of nature, I was like an early explorer, finding all these wonders for the first time. I would run home and want to share my finds. I still do. I remember most vividly the trips we made to the Ozarks to visit Aunt Dolly and her family in the hollows of southern Missouri hill country: trees, bluffs and caves. After growing up in the flat cornfields of Illinois, it was like magic. I remember the two camping trips I made with my mother and sister to Starved Rock State Park, along the Illinois River. I was allowed to walk the trails alone, though I was only eight and ten at the time. I found deep-sided canyons with exotic foliage hanging off the walls — ferns and who knows what else. I remember thinking those places the most perfect and wonderful sights I had ever seen. I wandered and pushed through the thick brush, meeting no one on the trails, which petered off into bush. What highs I felt. I still remember the rush.

When I drove along the Oregon coast twenty years later and saw Humbug State Park, it hit me: this is like Starved Rock! I lived there for two years before coming to see Vancouver Island. Driving through Gold-stream Park I thought, This is where I belong! I felt that rush and knew I was where I wanted to be – among rocks, waterfalls, vaulted rock faces covered with ferns, stonecrops and moss – rampant growth, lush and rich and moist.

Ron calls me "the larcenous landscaper"; I think of myself more as an opportunistic landscaper. I use what is readily available and tinker with it as the years go by. Slowly my little piece of heaven changes, as I recreate the enchanted places of my childhood and invent new wondrous areas. Always trying to find new kinds of enchantment. Along the way I have learned to read the land, observing the drainage or lack thereof, taking advantage of hot pockets created naturally by the lay of the land and vegetation, and creating special growing pockets by imitating nature, using berms and hedges, fences and raised planting boxes. Mostly I take advantage of what is already there.

Now that I don't have the physical energy or strength to overcome Mother Nature, I discover more and more labour-saving ways to garden. I see the problems way ahead and avoid them. In my vigorous days I quite loved spending days and days sitting in the sun, pulling weeds and crumbling the soil. Now I can't do that, so I find other ways of creating my visions. And I have become rather superstitious: If something wants to grow somewhere, I feel a compulsion to work around it and make it part of the ever-changing scene. This in itself has led to some most interesting and beautiful developments.

Now I will end with a confession that tells it all. I went to Butchart Gardens once about twenty-eight years ago and found it boring; I never went back. I always keep fairly quiet about this, as it's not a popular position. I do encourage my guests to go see Butchart if they show interest, but I never go with them. What I do enjoy with those same guests is stopping my car along the roadside in Mill Bay and walking them down to the seldom-seen old stone bridge. We pass water pools with moss hanging down, waterfalls, bushes and trees forming a vaulted roof over one of the Seven Wonders of the World – the deep, deep large black pool "with no bottom." I never say a word, just listen to their gasps and oohs and aahs. I love giving these spectacular tours. No one gardens these places, and no one charges a fee.

Love, Carol

CAROL'S JOURNAL

I really don't want to go to the doctor's this morning. It is a combination of things: dreading starting something new and fear of a new drug that may not work or may make me worse. Because I don't know what caused this disease in the first place, I fear everything. The only thing I can really control is what I put in my mouth. The closer the time comes for taking a new drug, the more I think, "It can't work. The miracle I want is not this." I have had my hopes up so many, many times that something could cure me, but still a tiny voice says, "Maybe, maybe."

I am very allergic to most medication, or so sensitive to it that the "cure" is often worse than the problem. However, my cholesterol count is way too high

and I can no longer keep it down with my really radical diet, as I did in the past, so have to go on medication next week for that. My blood pressure has continued to rise, despite all efforts to control it in natural ways. All of these side problems could be worsened by the CFS, but still have to be addressed.

❦

I've had to reassess a lot of things since becoming ill and losing my strength and independence. Before I got ill I knew I could always take care of myself and mine. I was willing to work harder than anybody, and did — I was not shy about what jobs I took on. Since developing this strange illness I have been misjudged a lot by family and friends and especially by "the system." Yet I know I have not been treated badly compared to others, and that's because I had a solid upbringing, good education and intelligence, and healthy self-esteem. My recent experience has given me a great deal of care and empathy for the people in our society who are not well equipped: the not so bright, not so healthy, not well brought up, not educated, etc. Somehow for a society to survive, places have to be made for everyone to live with dignity.

I am thankful that I lived in this community long enough and got to know plenty of people before I got sick. There were enough friends and acquaintances that some would help and stick by me.

July 31st
Dear Carol,
It is raspberry weather: clear skies, warm but not sweltering. I should be out there, moving down the rows, filling yogurt containers with ripe red berries. But this summer there are barely enough for a nibble. Our

renters, with the best of intentions, cut the canes to about knee height, just right for the chickens to strip.

When we first bought this farm there was a huge raspberry patch just by the side of the house. We moved in here on a July first, raspberry season, and about a week later Rudy's mother, father and grandmother arrived for a visit. His father was anxious to help us get going on our renovations. He was still wiry and alert, coughing his usual hacking cough, a cigarette with an unstable length of ash hanging from his lips. He moved with sluggishness, but we didn't recognize it then. A year later he died of lung cancer. I picked gallons of berries that year, thinking of him. Two years later my sister-in-law had just died – a poet who breathed metaphor and whose backhand humour always caught me by surprise. I was pregnant that July, afraid that I was way too crazy to actually become a mother. I picked those berries thinking of Susan and the baby in me who I would name for her if she was a girl.

Rudy moved the raspberry patch a few years later and now he says it needs to be moved again. When I think of the first patch I think of that bittersweet mixture – the sun warming me to physical comfort, being cushioned by the reassurance of doing something useful when in fact picking raspberries is licence to drift and dream, and the undercurrent of grief, momentarily forgotten, remembered again and again forgotten. Though I never said it, I hoped that moving the raspberries might ward off more death in the family. I associate the new location more with summer chatter, a friend picking in an adjoining row. And with Cicely madly picking to sell to the local store.

For me this is about the seasonal layering of time. I spend so much

time obsessively trying to get things done, working to one deadline or another, that I need plants to anchor me. When the February daphne blooms fragrant pink it says "Pay Attention — if you don't, you'll miss me." Now there is a wild delphinium outside the window, a crazy lavender cross, and each day it has fewer buds and flowers, more seed pods forming, like summer's clock ticking off the days. The plants' moments ground me, when I let them, to their time, this time, this very moment.

The paradox is that the garden teaches me that time is embracing as well as fleeting. Years ago, I started wild rugosa roses from seed I ordered from Abundant Life Seeds. After a year or two the plants that had survived were big enough to plant out along the driveway. They're tough, so they did OK, even competing with the grass. Then slowly, over the years, they grew mature enough to bloom. In June I noticed that one bush had white flowers. All the rest were magenta. It bothered me. I kept wondering should I dig it out, grow a new one to replace it. Then I saw that another bush was blooming white, too. I figured it was beyond my control then, and I moved into peace. I am prouder of that line of shrub roses than almost anything else — as if they were children that I birthed and watched grow into adulthood. The rose story is a good antidote to my impatience.

At the moment I'm struggling more with being out of sync with time. After so many months away it is clear that several things need moving. I want to do it right away, but I don't water faithfully enough to take the chance, so I will wait for fall.

I have been studying the architecture of Queen Anne's lace. They grow like unfurling gothic cathedrals, complete with pointed arches and flying buttresses. I continue to be amazed that I can walk past something for years before I actually see it. And it excites me that there is always more to see.

The wild cherries are almost done but the Japanese plums are just now coming on.

How many lilies now?

Love, Dorothy

August 9th   *11 water lilies*

Dear Dorothy,

I have been sending copies of our letters to my dear cousin Evelyn, who lives in Florida. She wrote recently:

"I love your and Dorothy's letters. We always had a big garden. White potatoes, sweet potatoes, spinach, peas, green beans, tomatoes, asparagus, kohlrabi, watermelon, strawberries. Then mother had about 1000 gladiolas. She added more each year. She planted about 100 bulbs every two weeks, so we had blooms over a long period of time. We had peonies, lily-of-the-valley, roses, columbines – so many plants I can't remember them all. There was something we called 'ground cherries,' which were like seeds in a little paper bag with six sides."

Evelyn's parents would have been gardening like this in the 1910s through the 1920s. Likely there have been two or three generations since then who have no gardening experience like that in our childhood.

When I was in a nature bookstore recently, the owner commented that many of us have lost our connection with the land. People come to his store for gardening books, but they think they have to start with "essentials" like a $200 jumpsuit to even go out in their yards. He said they don't really have any idea that gardening means getting down and dirty, crumbling the soil and watching nature. What he observes may be partly true, but just the fact that people want to buy gardening books indicates that something is brewing on a large scale.

Your description of Queen Anne's lace made me think of a story about it. Once I went collecting with a friend. It was a misty and muggy day. She carefully chose the heads that were particularly beautiful to her – all curled up they resemble the hairstyles of women in the 1890s, upswept with loosely straggling curls around the neckline. Because the weather was turning really foul, we gathered quickly and jumped into the car and drove home. By the time we reached the house, some of her prize specimens were slowly uncurling. Ten minutes later they had spread out into the rather flat lacy "doilies." You see Queen Anne's Lace has a built-in protective mechanism. The most dry, lifeless plant, when rained on, will pull up its stalks and sort of curl upwards, much like an umbrella closing upside down, so as to protect the seeds. In dry weather the "dead" seed head will spread out its spines, ready to drop its precious seeds. Nature magic.

In 1931 or 1932, after spending her childhood in California in a foster home, my mother joined her sisters in Kansas and Missouri. She tried to help them in the strawberry fields, but she found the work very hard. She recalls that they all covered their bodies carefully from the sun, not to protect themselves from dangerous overexposure but because being sun-tanned was a sign that you worked outside – something to be ashamed of. Being lily white was a sign of sophistication and wealth.

When I was growing up, people had already stopped growing their own food, even when they had yards to garden in. Now I can grow only token amounts of food, so I find places where I can buy fresh, locally grown garden produce. The Flea Market that's held at the Cobble Hill Hall every Sunday morning is one such place. There I met Beatrice, a woman in her eighties, descended from pioneers in this area. She grows a tremendous amount of food on her small acreage, so much that every week she can sell huge luscious lettuces for twenty-five cents each. She holds a vast amount of trial-and-error information from her years of gardening. How to tap it? She is reluctant to answer my "dumb" questions, but I get some interesting plants from her.

The bees are looking fantastic. In the cold, cold rain we had for those few days, they took care of business and seem no worse for wear. You must come and look at them again.

Love, Carol

August 19th
Dear Carol,
Such a strange August: thick pelting rains and low skies. It seems too soon for fall and yet it feels like fall. The late spinach I just planted is happy. The great leafy tomato plants have resolutely green tomatoes.

I think back on earlier years when I spent every day canning and freezing, the blue enamel canner steaming up the house, earwigs crawling out from peach pits hoping to sidle into the flour, me running to the store for more plastic bags, more canning lids. Have we given up eating? Or just thinking about eating? As I spend hours at the computer every day writing about traditional paper in India and Nepal, I feel like I'm doing another kind of preserving this summer — writing against a world changing so fast it feels like quicksand. I take breaks to pick too-fat zucchini (which don't care if there's sun), to admire the zinnias which have grown into a crazy jumble, and to eat blackberries along the driveway. A few days ago I thought I'd do a real pick — for jam or vinegar — but the energy ebbed and I'm back to grazing.

I have been thinking about evolution. When we bought this farm twenty years ago, there was a young bigleaf maple behind the sheds, and beyond that a plastic greenhouse. I tried for one or two years to start brassicas in the greenhouse, but the light was poor, probably because the maple had shot up almost as tall as the sheds. After another year or so the plastic got brittle and began to scatter shards everywhere. We took the greenhouse down and hauled away the rotting logs at its base. The area had a sad, derelict look.

Near the maple is a large round rock, dropped like a dinosaur egg by a receding glacier. It was overgrown with blackberries, and after years of impatience with them, I hauled them out. Then I could see the wonderful grey grit of the rock and the succulents that had nestled in its crevices all those years. I planted a red-leaf Japanese maple over the rock and later moved a volunteer Japanese plum and a purple smoke tree back there.

This small area began to be a shady purple glade, a spot that is cool and self-sufficient. This summer I added another Japanese maple, one we traded in exchange for pasturing a friend's horse. This one has wispy green leaves, tinged red. Set behind the rock, it can stretch across to whisper to the small purple maple beneath the overarching native maple, which in twenty-two years has developed a massive mottled trunk and is twice the height of the sheds.

There has never been much of a plan for the area — just a sense of purple and the realization that it was becoming very shady. I am not much of a garden designer, since plants always surprise me. I like that they will grow their own way, not bending to my will. They will steadfastly reveal themselves regardless of the misguided plans I have for them, or quietly remove themselves if I've misunderstood them.

Years ago I wanted gardens that other people would admire. Now I think of gardens as moments of pleasure, passages that bring me to a sharp consciousness of the moment. Last summer I made an intimate little sitting spot with a chair set against a corner of the house where several varieties of thyme creep between flagstones. It's just outside the window where I write, a perfect spot for a break, but I have to walk out the back door and around to get there. Usually when I want to sit outside with a snack I just crouch in the sunny doorway of the toolshed across from the kitchen door. With a fig tree growing on one side (with tiny figs that rarely ripen) and young santolina on the other, it's not a bad spot, but definitely not magazine material.

Weeks ago I wrote about my wild delphinium outside this window. There are only three blooms left. All the rest have formed seeds. In a few days when they dry out some more I will scatter them where they might be happy. Beyond them the apples are reddening up now. This particular variety tastes better after the first frost, so they have a long way to go, but they speak to me of time turning. Bittersweet, this end of summer. I am hoping for golden silent days in September, perhaps my favourite time.

How are the bees doing in all this rain?

Much love, Dorothy

August 21st 4 *water lilies*

Dear Dorothy,

It is 5:45 a.m. and the sun is not up but the clouds in the east are pink and grey. At this time of morning there is that special light that makes the garden magical. I quietly slipped onto the deck, looking out onto the boulder area, the flower garden and beyond to the wisteria arbour and orchard. My chest had a tight ache because of the beauty. I find myself getting panicky because the season is closing. The "body-snatcher" squash is living up to my name for it; when you pull the giant leaves away they are almost pulsating with growth and life. All that growth from one little volunteer plant!

I picked the first fully ripened seed from the cosmos. They go from seed to seed in less than four months. The large feral apple at the bottom of the orchard already is ripe. I hate that: ripe apples make the summer seem over. But we are stepping and sliding on fallen apples and they're attracting wasps, so I have to admit it's time to pick them. I thought this year I would finally retrieve my food dryer from the upper shelf in Ron's workshop, but I know it will stay up there because I have no new energy. When we first lived here, I made my own apple butter, sweetened only with concentrated pineapple juice. The first couple of years I made so much that I gave lots away and still Ron complained about freezer space. I don't have that kind of energy now.

☙

I have been thinking about gardening, nature study and closeness to the earth, and remembering what that bookstore owner said about jumpsuit-clad prospective gardeners. North Americans may be estranged from the earth and nature, but this is a short-lived thing. A new devotion to the earth is being found, not just here but among individuals all over the world. The heartening thing is that this one-person-at-a-time change is growing at exponential rates.

When I first came to Canada and lived on Saltspring Island, it was regular practice for local residents to bring their garbage along on the ferry to Vancouver Island and, in the middle of the channel, get out of their cars, open the trunk and dump the garbage bags over the side – with no shame or repercussions. Try to imagine this now. Everyone I know has slowly changed to composting, recycling and voluntarily stopping all open burning. We are all becoming very, very aware of the earth, like blind men given sight.

I see much television devoted to gardening, nature study, preservation of wildlife and conservation of the earth's resources. There are exposés on worldwide pollution and reports of mind-boggling clean-up projects ranging from industries in Scandinavia which use each other's wastes, to composting toilets in developing countries. All kinds of

people have been working for many years to solve world problems without tipping the balance of nature. This news never makes headlines. I see evidence of more and more people wanting their earth clean, beautiful and healthy. Whether there are enough people caring quickly enough to save us is another question.

⪡

Kathy was over yesterday. I couldn't help myself and proudly showed her this year's "accidental" squash. It is the largest single squash plant I've ever seen. It has commandeered too much of Ron's lawn. His face goes all tight as I continue to put hay underneath the many growing heads. It has grown all the way from the flower garden to the roadside apple tree.

Kathy and I used sticks to pull aside leaves, trying to count the number of squash heads. Kathy thought there were twenty. I think twelve. Sure, there are more, but unless the season continues for a long time they will not grow. Kathy sees twenty because it is my squash; in her yard she would see twelve. We always see another person's garden by focussing on what we do not have in our own.

Kathy said, "I don't understand it. You must have wonderful soil." Her garden is on river-bottom soil. I started six years ago, on a four-inch layer of enriched clay, a thicker layer of unenriched clay and a layer of hardpan. Six feet down there is bedrock. So I said, "Well, Kathy, you know how I work. I carefully balance the pH of the soil and add just the correct amount of fertilizer, making sure the nitrogen-phosphorus-potash levels are perfect for squash." She cracked up. She knows me too well. In the pottery studio, years ago, I made glazes. I had studied the chemical analysis and formulation of glazes, but I found trial and error much more to my liking. The results were fantastic. Likewise, I have studied gardening books, I've resolved to use technical advice, I've even thought about putting magnesium on my yellowed-leaf lilac, Ruth. I am still thinking about it. Maybe the lilac felt my good intentions because she perked up, looked great and bloomed like mad this year. Or maybe it was time, Mother Nature, the steer manure, compost and hay?

The bees are fine and I have many good photos of them. Today we are renting a video camera for recording the garden, pond and bees. We hope to do this once a year. I hope the weather clears up.

Love, Carol

CAROL'S JOURNAL

I had a very bad experience at the hospital last week getting the intravenous magnesium. It caused some very scary flushing and constriction of the throat, which brought on an adrenaline rush. I thought I would pass out. The nurse who was monitoring me yelled at me to describe what was happening but I couldn't speak. My blood pressure went up (the usual fear with magnesium is that one's blood pressure goes down) and finally they put me in a cold corner with a small window open and I soaked my blouse to help me cool off. I just about gave up on the IV because I was so upset, but stuck it out because I knew I would be very fearful to go next time. That night neither Ron nor I even attempted sleep until 2 a.m., and then I slept only in bits and pieces.

I've had trouble taking the magnesium, but lately I have had more energy, or maybe it's more strength. But I still get exhausted so quickly that I can't go out alone at all. When the exhaustion hits, I have to lie down immediately.

After the bad IV I had, I had another one this week that was even worse. I had to leave without getting the treatment. The nurse who tried to get the needle in botched it twice, once letting the drip into my wrist, which created a swelling of liquid and blood. She bandaged that wrist and tried a vein in my other hand but couldn't get the needle in there either. She finally called another nurse but by then I had already been there over an hour so could not see being there for two more hours if the second nurse hit the right place. I gave up and went outside, trying to walk off the tension while waiting for Ron to take me home.

I'm not certain why it seems to be harder and harder for me to get a "clean" IV. Regardless, I've decided to space the treatments every nine days rather than every seven days.

I love to look at the yard, so much so that for the first time that I can remember, I dread winter. I can't stand that this beauty will change.

August 28th

Dear Carol,

It has been a summer of visitors, all from the east. Few of them have spent much time in gardens. They marvelled at how asparagus grow, at how a real strawberry tastes, at how ripe peaches look airbrushed on the tree. They have the misguided notion that if you live in the country, you are always peaceful and in tune. I say, "Well, if you're in the country and your head is still noisy, at least you know where the noise is coming from." My head is very noisy these last few days.

What is clear to me is that the garden can be as much an arena to work out conflicts as anywhere else. In the very early days, the garden was a place where I felt unsure and overwhelmed. Rudy had gardened some before we moved here, and he somehow thought I should know instinctively what to do. I didn't. We'd moved to the country with the idea of "living off the land," as we said in those days. He even had a gun, though I'm not sure what he thought he'd shoot. He sold it later, when he was able to admit it scared him. Vegetables were what scared me a bit, but over time I got used to them. I do remember those first gardens when I didn't know you had to plant scads of peas to get enough to eat – I'd harvest six pods and treat them like gold.

Eventually we bought this farm. It had a big vegetable garden and over the years we kept making it bigger. I spent more and more time growing things I thought I should and canning things we never got around to eating. Finally I rebelled. I stopped trying to prove what a good farm wife I was. I stopped trying to deny that I was an urban transplant trying to do an impossible balancing act – mothering a kid, working in my studio, reading until my eyes popped out of my head and gardening and freezing and canning. Things got easier. Around that time, Rudy gave me a watering can for my birthday. It was a beautiful English watering can and I still use and appreciate it, but at the time I nearly threw it in his face. I wanted some sign that there was more in my life than the albatross garden.

I wasn't the only one who was a little nuts in those days. We had a milk cow then. Rudy kept feeding her huge amounts of grain, which meant she produced obscene amounts of milk which we had trouble selling, and she had chronic mastitis. I finally said, "Stop."

It seems a long time ago, those battles. These days I feel more like I have an ebb and flow relationship with the garden. There have been summers when I didn't do much of anything, followed by summers when I planted wheat for bread and grew five or six varieties of dried beans. We got home too late to plant them this year and I miss them. Shelling them is like gathering jewels. They are such miraculous energy storehouses with their compact roundness, their sheen and pattern. The pods are marvellous too. When their fleshiness dries, they become rattly husks. My favourites are matte blue-black on the outside with cozy nests inside, one for each bean, like faded silk.

This summer I have gardened as much on paper, in these letters to you, as I have in the real garden. It happens like that. I am past guilt, at least most of the time. One way I came to peace was by planting what I love to look at and love to eat. In the vegetable garden that means radicchio rather than carrots. We are plagued with carrot rust fly here. Besides, carrots are cheap and always available at the farmers' market. The radicchio, an Italian endive, is not so readily available. After the first frost the leaves turn ruby red, some varieties marbled with white, some with a purply green. I start cutting the heads in November, and by January or February they send up tiny new heads, providing greens all winter. They have a strong flavour, fantastic with olive oil and a few roasted pine nuts. We have a paradoxical climate here – corn salad, Belgian endive, mizuna and various mustard greens in the winter, but few ripe tomatoes in summer.

I love the garden at this season when the sun heats my back, but gently. Kneeling in cold naked soil planting the first peas in early spring is no great joy to me. I lack faith. The ground stretches, ready; I put in the seeds, but the vision of staked peavines loaded with pods is thin. Then the cats run over the newly planted beds, the chickens get in if someone leaves the gate open, the weather turns foul and nothing comes up. I prefer this florid weedy time when everything is overspilling its boundaries.

This summer we have walnuts on three trees, two bearing for the first time, one of them a scrawny little thing. Those neat shiny walnuts hanging in pairs remind me of the balls on a young male cat. Years ago when we planted a walnut orchard, it was like a covenant with the land, a promise to plant things that took years to fruition. I didn't know if we would be here long enough to see nuts on the trees but here we are.

The Steller's jays are back. Yesterday I saw one sitting in a hazelnut tree, hammering a nut with its beak, the green hazelnut a brilliant contrast to the jay's sapphire feathers. That was the signal I've been waiting for. I know from experience: if you don't act fast when you see the first jay, the nuts will all be gone. The hazelnuts are wonderful, all wrapped in husks like pale green ruffled tutus. They leave a fragrant stickiness on my hands when I pick them. I pick whatever I can reach from the ground, leaving the rest for the jays – a kind of tithe to the wild things that I learned from a farmer more than twenty years ago. I let them sit until the husks dry out, then the shells turn rich brown and by December they are ready to eat.

Writing this has smoothed out some of the noise in my head. That's good. The wild delphinium seeds outside the window look ready to scatter. I will close for today.

Love, Dorothy

September 3rd   *4 water lilies*

Dear Dorothy,

I loved your last letter, and found myself often nodding in agreement. You've inspired me to attempt some winter salad greens again. Could I have some seeds from the radicchio? Before I became ill I ate from my garden and greenhouse year round at Briarwood. Here I haven't attempted winter vegetables yet, except the first season I scattered corn salad seeds once but they didn't take. Ron mows too much. At Briarwood, corn salad grew reluctantly in a raised bed but self-seeded along the pathways, as if it did not like comfort and care. So I scattered its seed everywhere and it materialized with ease in the oddest places.

A friend of mine, Sherry, wants some input into how to landscape and garden in her new place. I am anxious to see her land because it is fertile ground for my imagination: New land to tinker with. First successes are so important for anyone wanting to grow food, so my first suggestion was, "Grow squash." The seeds are huge, the seedlings are huge and they make masses of beautiful, lush leaves. The amount of impressive growth from one plant is enough to make anyone beam. Beneath the leaves are the surprises. All winter long we bake squash for lunch, stuffing them with onions, green and red pepper, basil and cheese. At this point I'm eager to make a list of "Easy Vegetables" for Sherry and will give you a copy. Maybe you would make a list for her too? (No more than three).

My favourite part of gardening, when I am able, is weeding and cultivating soil with my hands. This is where I can bliss out and let the world and its reality pass me by. Nothing else quiets me or puts me into relaxation quite like weeding and crumbling. Happiness for me is my lady gloves, a trowel, a cushion, a warmish but not hot day, and time and energy to head for the garden beds.

I also love to examine road cuts, looking at the layers of earth: topsoil, subsoil, clay, gravel. When I was about six or seven, my passion was to dig a cave. I only had a spoon to dig into the hillside, but that did not stop me. During a later summer I dug clay under a grape arbour. I don't know how I knew what it was, but I discovered its magical qualities and made clay things that dried in the sun. I guess my love of crumbling the soil and making pottery is the same thing. Both activities calm me and quiet my cluttered head.

⤛

I am beginning to make pear butter from the pears we picked from your tree. After last year's fiasco of craving local pears, watching them fall in yards unpicked and then not getting any at the farmers' market, I was geared up for pears this year. On our way back from your house, I noticed many more little stands along the road where everyone is selling their extra flowers, vegetables and fruit. I think this is wonderful. Farmer Horton has a little stand that says "PEARS."

Love, Carol

AUTUMN

September 22th

Dear Carol,

The pole beans, planted so late, are finally in full production. The fat green ones lie languid on the leaves like lizards in the sun or like one of Manet's fleshy ladies picnicking *sur l'herbe*. I envy them those moments of self-abandonment.

I thought I had been ruthless this year with the self-sown nasturtiums, but they have taken over. They sprawl everywhere, a profusion of orange and yellow-orange and red-orange – eye candy. The vines tumble and stretch and twine. In the last light of the evening they glow eerily when everything else has disappeared into dusky murk. There are other unasked-for gifts in another part of the garden: volunteer gourds – the clowns of the garden, joyously non-functional. There are fabulous ones with eccentric stripes and warts, as well as bi-tones: green-and-white, green-and-yellow, orange-and-green. I lined up five orange ones like the famous sumi-e painting of the five persimmons.

Reading about your love of soil reminds me that one reason I say I'm not really a gardener is because of my problem with soil. One of the things that drives me wild about gardening is the way my hands feel when soil dries on them. I walk around holding my fingers apart, longing for hand cream. I respond more to the look of soil than its feel. Last year when we drove across Oklahoma I was ecstatic over the terra-cotta soil just starting to sprout lines of grey-green seedlings – perfect complementary colours. And I loved the earthy ochre colour of the greasy riverbanks all around the Bay of Fundy, where the tides come in forever.

For me the best part of gardening is weeding rows of vegetables. It satisfies me to see the pure rhythm of each row when the weeds are gone. Each vegetable sings its own song; each variety has its own persona. The curly endive is all spiky ins and outs, the butter lettuce is buttery, the romaine stands like soldiers, the spinach is lobed like the lungwort lichen that hangs in the maples. I see the rows of vegetables as tapestry. In the days when I used to weave I kept the garden very orderly. These days things are more random and haphazard, more like the way I work with handmade paper. I don't think I knew this until you wrote about your potter's approach to soil.

My other favourite gardening activity is harvesting – piling tomatoes, zucchini and cucumbers into baskets and laying pink cosmos, electric zinnias and rose and white nicotiana on top. I am a natural hoarder – a quality I don't admire in myself – but the abundance of the garden makes it easy to be lavish and expansive. This in itself is a gift of the garden.

I have been thinking about your question about easy vegetables. Nasturtiums pop into my head first, but are they vegetables? They germinate easily and they're so beautiful in salads, especially scattered with chive and borage flowers. And I love their peppery taste. Next I think of kohlrabi, particularly the purple ones because I like their colour, though I think the green ones may grow faster. All the brassicas germinate easily. I love to eat raw kohlrabi in soy sauce, oil and vinegar.

Potatoes are great; some years we've grown yellow, blue, pink and reddish-brown varieties. Digging them is like an Easter egg hunt and they taste so much better straight from the garden. Well that's three, but I'm not sure it's a sensible list of three

⟸

I have been photographing the fruit in the trees, noticing how each variety has its own colour scheme. The Cox's orange has russety leaves that echo the warmth of the apples; the Northern Spy leaves are a gentle grey-green in tune with the ghostly pink-tinged fruit. Today I photographed the medlars. They are a strange medieval fruit, small round brown things with four tusk-like spurs at the blossom end. After they are picked, they have to blet, which means soften, in fact begin to rot a bit. The medlar tree is a visual treat. Soon its leaves will turn bright shades of red and orange.

How wonderful to still have water lilies. This is such a poignant time of year – golden ripe rotting bee-buzzed fullness heightened by the consciousness of bare branches and dried frosted bracken waiting in the wings.

Love, Dorothy

October 1st   *Cold again, 42 degrees*
Dear Dorothy,
My three votes for three easy-to-grow vegetables go to squash, tomatoes and chard. I know it sounds crazy to list tomatoes in our climate, but I have never had a year in which I didn't get tomatoes. I always get at least

a few ripened on the vine (or lots), and the rest I bring in green and they ripen in the house, a few at a time. They are so easy to germinate, they self-seed like crazy and every sucker you snap off can be stuck into the soil and it grows. I love such easy plants. Last fall seed magic happened with the compost and its pile of rotted tomatoes. Despite cold winter rains, snow, freezing and constant dampness, the seeds were ready to sprout. (So much for the instructions on how to store seeds, huh?) In the spring, tomatoes by the hundreds sprouted in the flower boxes, in the beds, everywhere that compost had been spread. I have to give a gold star to tomatoes just for their tenacity, regardless of whether our summers get hot enough to ripen them all.

I know that chard is not a flashy character in the vegetable kingdom, but it germinates in the damp cold and and tastes somewhat like spinach in early spring. When spinach is bolting and nasty tasting, chard continues to grow and produce large, fat, succulent green-and-white stalks. My friend Heinz, a great cook, came one day "to cook for us the chard." He proceeded to cut off only the green leafy parts, discarding the succulent stalks. Then he overcooked the leaves and pureed them with butter and seasonings. It was delicious. When I told him the stalks were also quite tasty, he was greatly amazed. His face wrinkled with dismay. "You eat those? We did not use them back home." (Germany, pre- and post-World War II.)

☙

I wrote a letter to my aunt in Missouri, thinking I might elicit interesting gardening/farming experiences in reply. In the past I've doubled up with laughter at her stories of the farm. Anyway, I thought you would enjoy her answer to my long paragraphs of questions on her background with gardening and farming in the Ozarks from the late 1920s through the 1940s: "Work up the ground good, plant seeds or plants, hoe them when needed and keep the weeds down. Homer and I used fertilizer on everything we raised."

She would have been a good one to keep state secrets. Actually she entered farming when she and her younger sister were released from the orphanage in the early 1920s to her uncle's dirt-poor farm in Missouri. She and her sister were expected to hoe and weed four acres of grapes and five acres of strawberries. Apparently the whole countryside was gossiping about the way her uncle worked the two of them. Her answer to this is, "Well, you can see that it didn't hurt us. At eighty-four and eighty-five, we are still on our feet."

Two of Ron's sons came by last night. I sent them into my little study, the only place I could find to store the giant "body-snatcher" squash. The first one in said, "Whoa – what are these? They look like those things from *Cocoon*. What would you do with these?" (He is even too young to remember *Invasion of the Body Snatchers*.) When I suggested that they will feed us this winter, he said that we should send them to Bosnia. I guess this is the modern version of "send them to the starving children of India." Neither of these boys was raised in families that garden. Each of them sees his surroundings so differently. One is greatly impressed by our gardens and woods and goes around in verbal ecstasy. There is a "down the road" gardener in that boy. Seeing and being thrilled is the first stage.

CAROL'S EASY SQUASH

Cut into reasonable-sized pieces for baking.

Clean out the seeds and rub a tiny amount of butter in each seed cavity.

Fill with Carol's stuffing.

Bake at 350 degrees in water in a baking pan, covering lightly at first with foil.

When done (test with a fork), sprinkle lightly with skim-milk cheese, letting it melt.

SQUASH FILLING

Onions, thinly sliced and lightly precooked in the microwave.

Red and green peppers cut into chunks.

Mix these up with lots of basil and mound up in seed cavities.

I cook up many at one time, refrigerating the leftovers and reheating them in the microwave at lunchtime. I vary what goes into the squash cavity depending on what I have on hand.

In this long, extended summer I have been watching the garden and the birds with great intensity. I quietly spy on the small goldfinches in the cosmos beds. They dart up and down so quickly, making the cosmos appear to be moving in the wind. The tinkling sounds and beautiful questioning calls sound joyful and happy. I know they are eating something in the cosmos and assume that it is the seeds. They stand precariously on the flowers and move as on a roller coaster with the swaying stems. Yesterday I was in the right place at the right time and focussed on one bird on one flower. After he left I examined the flower and confirmed that he ate the seeds, still in their immature, soft stage with golden pollen stamens. I couldn't help but wonder about the gold of the goldfinch and the gold of the pollen. This is only my second year of growing cosmos. Without them I would never have seen the goldfinches in action. For all my fifty-six years they have been living out their mysterious lives, cavorting and twittering, generation after generation, until finally I see them.

In 1967, on Saltspring Island, I signed up for a course called "Eating from Nature," taught by Ingrid Temmel, who emigrated from Germany with her artist husband. They had been trapped by the war, he in a Russian prison camp and she in Germany. Because of the lost years of their twenties, they had their family late: five children, the last one born to her at age forty-three. Ingrid had advanced degrees in botany and was truly brilliant. She walked our small class through the woods and we ate wild things. This is how she lived and raised her children. They milked goats and made black rye bread. She was so practical and down to earth. Our close friendship ended abruptly two years later when she was killed in a freak auto accident. I still mourn her and regret that I did not continue to walk the woods and eat all those wild things.

She has been dead over twenty-five years and I feel her influence, her presence, almost more as time goes on. Your first letter in June reminded me of her again. For me she was that person of your daydreams who sits in

the small shack overlooking the reedy marsh, watching the blackbirds light on the cattails.

☙

The bees are changing formation now, showing more of their four beautiful combs. The undulating bottoms of the combs glow with a pink/coral/golden hue. The bees seem to flatten themselves up between the combs. There are only three slots in which they can fit, and not all can make it there. Once in a while one drunkenly wanders around alone on the unfilled comb, then returns to the clump of the hive. It is so rainy and cold this morning. We make our trip each morning to check the bees, but with much more apprehension these days.

Love, Carol

CAROL'S JOURNAL

I turn fifty-seven this month. I last had a normal life when I was forty-six. My life then was filled with work, people, pottery and plants and animals. Now I am considered an older woman, but in my head I'm still forty-something because it is as if I have been in limbo, waiting, waiting. The tests at Johns Hopkins only include people up to age fifty. For the very first time I feel "past it." To think I might not qualify for their trials because of my age. I can understand why they would draw lines, but somehow it makes me feel worth less than nothing.

☙

I have about two hours of fairly OK *energy and muscle in the afternoon. If I use it, I am finished early. If I can take it very, very slowly I can last until 4 p.m. or a bit later. I have gone back to acceptable sleep (thank goodness). Naps from 9 p.m. until midnight, then one good sleep for two or three hours, then naps for the rest, with wide-awake periods of thirty minutes and longer.*

❧

It's taken years for me to understand that my body actually stops digesting anything for hours if I am too fatigued or stressed, and this results in irritable bowel, pain, gas, constipation — and on and on. Early on in this disease, before anyone twigged that something was grossly wrong, I kept losing weight while eating lots of good food. Now I know it's because nothing was really digesting. I hardly remember that frightening period of my life (about nine years ago), except I remember being fearful to step on the scale.

October 4th

Dear Carol,

Did I write about the fragrance of hazelnuts a few weeks ago? This week I have been picking walnuts. The trees are such sheltering umbrellas, their scale is so grand, even though they are still young. Everything about them is rich and fat and generous: the stems that link the divided leaves, the awkward new growth and the nuts themselves. As I was picking I felt surrounded by a fragrant cloud, all piney and lemony at the same time.

Rudy gave me a great basket of mixed narcissus bulbs, a mounded heap of dried papery forms. So much promise. I wish I enjoyed planting them more. I tend to put them in the grass where I hope they will be happy and spread. Some do; some disappear. The difficulty is cutting through the matted surface and penetrating deep enough in this hard soil. Hard work but worth it if they come through.

It's now October 25 and I've been to Texas and back. I thought I would get this off to you before I left but things got too crazy. Now that I'm back I'm feeling low and overwhelmed. I had thought I was immune, after all these years, to the grey-sky blues, but I've really got them this week. Texas was so warm and sunlit. In the ten days I was away there's been a shift from the feeling of fall fruition and roundness to the inward-turning days when the world goes dark and sodden like some great festering compost heap. I harvested the tomatoes before I left since the nights were getting cold. Usually they last well into December, slowly ripening. This fall they are turning a mottled brown and then mould appears in snowy drifts.

Today I called a landscaper who will come to doctor my perennial border, something I have only dreamt about before. I have often envied the great English gardening ladies with their hired gardeners. Maybe with some help I can have a perennial border that gives pleasure without requiring great pain. It went from manageably chaotic to beyond coping while we were gone last year. I am hoping the landscaper can help me dig it and rethink it – plant shrubs interspersed with the day lilies, peonies and Siberian iris; pull out the phlox which spread like wildfire. These are about the only perennials the deer don't eat. In the last few years the true lily bulbs have tantalized me with their swelling buds, only to have them nipped by the deer.

We have a proud young buck with new-sprouted antlers hanging around lately. He stands almost at the doorway, checking to see if Rudy remembered to put the netting over the grapes, which some deer nearly stripped a few months ago. He is so very beautiful and so infuriating, leaping the orchard fence with angelic lightness.

~

I was struck by your mention of your friend Ingrid, who taught you about eating from the woods. I have two old ladies who are always with me. One of them, Peg, gave us the tiny red grapes, sweet and abundant, that grow by the kitchen door. Last year the renters didn't prune them, so there was double growth this summer and an unbelievable crop of grapes. Their weight pulled the fascia board off the shed they grow on, so now we have the vine propped up with two-by-fours. In a little while I'll prune them back and try to exert a bit more control. Peg also gave me a pale yellow peony with translucent single petals. It blooms in the still stark days of early spring, long before anything else, like a spectacular preview of coming attractions.

Bea Palmer was my real mentor. We met her when she sold us a few of her black karakul sheep. They moved through her fields like unicorns, heads held imperiously on gracefully arched necks. Her woods were full of wildflowers that she had dug and transplanted. Her vegetables grew in the neatest raised rectangles. I had so little gardening experience then that I hardly knew how to look at her gardens or what questions to ask, but I will always remember the sense of the garden wisdom she had accumulated from season after season of watching her plants grow.

We are planning to press some apples and pears this weekend, and we'll try to make grape juice. That will be a first. Writing this has cheered me up.

Love, Dorothy

October 31st *Cold, bright and frosty*
26 degrees

Dear Dorothy,

I am sitting in my office as usual, but now I have a wonderful large window looking out onto the deck that is teeming with birds. Engulfing the railing are cascara, wild crabapples and the splendid wild rose bush, now two storeys tall. I walked outside to check the thermometer and the quail didn't take any notice of me. Usually they treat me like the creature from the black lagoon. I wonder what was different this time.

I have been concentrating on the feral apples this year, taking group photos of their fruit and leaves. Ron hacked a path to each of the more hidden ones, and we watched them for ripeness, picking and tasting them, photographing them, drying slices and tasting them again. We're storing some, watching them intently to see if they are keepers. We know them so much better, having lived with them and cared for them for seven seasons. I have needed this year's luxury of time and peace to really enjoy them.

I've found that some of our volunteer apple trees actually produce more than one kind of apple. About half of them have many trunks, and I've seen two different crabapples where I thought one grew, and two quite different apples coming out of the same clump of trunks.

The Goat Apple put on an abundant crop, having finally come into its own. It took years to get over having its bark mercilessly stripped by the neighbour's goats (before I bought this land), and then being hemmed in by wild crabapples, which we cut down. This apple tastes exactly like the one we call the Rose Apple, which has produced fruit only once before

because it is recovering from a brush fire that damaged it as a sapling six summers ago. They are similar in colour, skin texture and lateness, but not in the way they grow. The Rose Apple acts like an oversized crabapple, whereas the Goat Apple grows like an ordinary full-size apple. But they both taste like a rose smells. If I close my eyes when chewing them, they taste like I am smelling a rose – an odd sensation – a taste instead of a smell.

My son came this weekend and saw the first group photo of feral apples. He started in with his droll humour about us becoming rather weird about the apple trees. I believe it's virtually impossible to communicate with a thirty-year-old. In my fifties, my appreciation of everything in nature is deeper, more personal and heartachingly compelling. I can't begin to tell this boy why these apples are so important.

☙

I am incorporating more labour-saving techniques in the garden. As my body changes and weakens I get very inventive, trying to stay out there and still keep my hand in. All of these shortcuts can make gardening easier for healthy people also. This winter I will compost on top of each of the planting beds. Make one compost, top it off and go to the next bed. I had a tug of war with Ron over where the compost piles were located before. He originally found the idea of them repugnant and put them back in the woods. This made them inaccessible to me, especially in winter, and because of the winter shade it was not a particularly good place for a healthy compost heap.

Now Ron is caught up and distracted learning the Internet, so I am taking over the composting. The first pile is only ten feet from the front deck, in my flower garden. I started by piling the kitchen waste right onto the prone and weather-beaten cosmos. Those stems will raise the whole heap slightly off the ground for a while. Soon I will have Ron bring me piles of manure, subsoil, sand and hay, placing them on that bed. With a small shovel handy at the door I can make the compost and it will look "just fine." Like fingerprints on my pottery, it is "part of the process." Each heap will have many hours of winter sun to warm it.

CAROL'S BEST COMPOST
(for a wettish climate)

(1) Pile rough branches on ground. I use cosmos stems, aster stems and trifid stems, which are sturdy but will break down eventually.

(2) On top of the rough stem base, place hay or anything like leaves, grass or smaller plants. These act to "tighten" the bottom of the "compost basket."

(3) Next to this pile, place mounds of manure, soil of any kind, sand and any composting treasures you have or can find.

(4) Pile or spread your kitchen waste on top of the rough stem base and cover it with some "dry substances" – soil, sand, hay, etc.

(5) After a couple of months, cover the compost with soil, hay, etc., and leave it till you need it.

The idea is to layer these substances, like making a trifle. At each stage you should end up with a dry topping to help prevent birds from

scratching it up too much. I find the raccoons and birds do dig around (because it is so richly full of worms), but I think of them as partners – they stir it up once in a while. We rake it back. I have never, ever smelled my compost piles and I have a nose that should be insured by Lloyds of London.

You notice I call this recipe "Carol's Best Compost." When I get lazy or tired or busy, or if I let other people "take out the compost," the kitchen waste just lies uncovered for long periods, building up a slimy, gooey substance. Eventually it gets covered, and it can still turn out to be wonderful. I've never found a failed compost; Nature will compost without my help. One busy year at Briarwood I found that one of the neglected piles of compost was a worm factory – thousands of fat, heavy, healthy earthworms. Wow, what an addition to my garden. I thought I had discovered gold.

My goal for this winter is to successfully compost in each of the planting beds, saving many steps of the process. This will allow me the pleasure of a winter garden project while saving my energy.

Another labour-saving practice I've begun is hanging the hand pruners at the front door so I carry them with me each time I walk around the yard. By pruning a little all winter – just five or ten cuts during each walk – pruning becomes a "non-job." I have discovered all kinds of wonderful things while winter pruning. For example, I can pick off most of the casings full of overwintering tent caterpillar eggs because they are so visible on the denuded branches, and so vulnerable. (Do you sense my glee?) I really see the bushes and trees when they are without their glamorous colourful leaves. Even though it is frosty or cold and rainy I am still out here. My garden is not left alone to heaven's cold and sodden advances.

~

November 3rd

I walked out to the bees, pruning another path to them. I stood directly under their hive and looked straight up, like looking at an upside-down plate rack. The bees are clustered up "inside" the larger space between the middle combs. I can see them moving slowly.

Love, Carol

November 10th

Dear Carol,

What weather! About a week ago on one of the icy cold days I watched maple leaves falling from the tree, clear yellows tinged orange, rimed with frost, like partly clenched fists, like open hands. The pile they created on the ground was illuminated by the first rays of the sun coming up from over in your direction. On mornings like that I walk as if on a highway, straight into the sun's magnetic gullet.

Two days ago, after endless rain, the air was warm and balmy. I was transfixed by the arbutus leaves fallen on the asphalt, unevenly mottled in muted greys and greens as if an artist had smudged them with powdered graphite. Lying on these leaves were drops of rain, perfect swollen lenses, aqueous jewels. In other places the yellow maple leaves were plastered to the road, all wet, translucent, like soaked tracing paper. This is a season of leaves.

When I was at Penland in North Carolina last year, a wonderful artist, Chris Allen-Wickler, showed slides of work she'd done by pasting small squares of paper on ivy growing on a wall. Each leaf turned brilliant reds and oranges except where she'd stuck the papers. When she removed the papers, there was a magnificent tension between the regularity of her "resists" and the organic chaos of the vine, a vital tapestry in green and red. She did another piece where she lined the broad steps of a university library with yellow leaves, arranged in orderly rows, each leaf held down by a stone. It was beautiful. Looking back now, it seems a foreshadowing of the rocks we saw placed on tree altars all over India.

Probably it is her inspiration that has made me look more carefully at the leaves on certain trees as they turn fall colours. You can see where some have been shaded by other leaves or by fruit, causing shadowy movements of muted colours. The colours here in British Columbia are rarely clear. Most often they are a symphony of modulated mud tones – orange mud, purple mud, ochre mud – but they sing. The medlar tree and a Korean dogwood are particularly good for these crazy quilt shadings. I photographed them today. I hope they turn out.

Today again it was crisp clear. The maples are almost bare. Their branches are etched on the sky with the pattern of the samaras, their winged seeds, still clinging up there. I sometimes confuse "samara" with "samsara," the Buddhist word for this illusory world. It *is* an illusory world, what can I say?

I am always picky about the weather I garden in. I walk in storms but I hate kneeling in wet, cold dirt. Instead I walk around, noticing spent flower stalks on perennials that need to be cut back and beds that should be put in order. Today I managed to do a bit of garden clean-up and that felt good. I also pruned the grape by the kitchen window. I'm not sure why I find the gnarly cut-off vines, hacked back to the heart, so beautiful, but I do.

Last weekend I picked the medlars. I have been thinking about two quotes that seem to connect. From Chaucer: "Till we be rotten can we not be rypen." And one of Yeats' Crazy Jane poems:

> But love has pitched his mansion in
> The place of excrement
> For nothing can be sole or whole
> That has not been rent.

Speaking of such things, I hope your recipe for compost inspires us. We tend to make the chaotic wet kind. Rototilled into the soil in spring, I'm sure it does a lot of good, but rarely have we produced the rich crumbly soil that I read about in books. Our culture tends to be so squeamish about rotting and excrement, and yet so much life is produced there. "Oh Shekinah (in Jewish mysticism the feminine principal of God immanent in the world), blet me" seems more relevant to me these days than to ask for blessing.

I am having a hard time this fall with the grey days. I feel sodden and heavy. The clear days pick me up again. Living here, I guess all I can hope for is some balance, a regular alternation between the grey and the gilded.

Love, Dorothy

Yesterday grew heavier and heavier on me until I had a feeling of not being able to breathe. I have had to take more Rivotril (an anti-spasmodic drug). I am sore in my hip joints and have unexplained knee bruising. I really feel a mess.

I felt so odd all day, culminating in a time of "freezing." It was so bad that I needed to lie in a hot tub, but the washer had been used so Ron had to run back and forth with hot water heated on the stove.

During the day I made a resolution to start a new energy-saving regime. Each day and each hour and each minute I am going to be conscious and watchful about overdoing it. I promise myself not to push myself, no matter how tempting. With this latest development I can't tell when I am getting close to overdoing it, so I must stop things far earlier on, just in case. I am cutting back on all conversation. I will not go to meetings or people's houses; I have no "have to's." I will lie down flat every hour, whether I need to or not. I will not go to Nanaimo for a long, long time. When I am tempted to just "do it," I will find alternatives: cancel it, mail it, courier it, have Ron phone it, forget it.

Last week Ron went to hear a doctor from New Zealand talk about the cause and "cure" for Myalgic Encephalomyelitis (this doctor hates the term Chronic Fatigue Syndrome and won't use it). It was so good for Ron to be in an auditorium filled with hundreds of people and to hear a doctor speak with empathy for people suffering from this physical disease / disorder. When he came home he was very thoughtful, stroking my hair and getting me things and rushing to arrange to send a blood sample to New Zealand for testing.

November 29th *Wet, dark 6 A.M.*

Dear Dorothy,

I am up from my bed after thirteen days of back trouble. It is still an ongoing battle to get over the severe pain, spasms and weakness caused by so much lying flat. I have had more than enough thinking time!

One thing I did was read over our letters. I enjoyed them immensely, and found that through the writing I've gained a better appreciation of my nature experiences. Memories called up to the surface give me insight: They are more precious than mementos sitting on my shelves. Since the days of exploring the canyons of the banks of the Illinois River, I continue to be amazed by life around me, wherever I am. This is the great gift in my life which has never really changed. Even in these dark days I watch the orb web spider living his life above my kitchen sink.

🖎

Ron and I both laughed a lot over your wonderful word "blet." We used it many times over the first days after reading your last letter. I feel a charlatan after reading your interpretation of my compost recipe. I have never ever had any compost come out as the experts profess it could be: rich crumbly soil. My best compost is always a surprise. I seldom leave the piles long enough, or do all the fussing with them that apparently is needed for the "perfect compost." They are of varying consistencies. The thing they all seem to do is make wonderful growing mediums, untidy and imperfect as they appear.

In 1977, when I had recently purchased Briarwood, I remember Kathy coming back from taking a gardening class. She had bought a wonderful little book, *The Postage Stamp Garden*. I have used raised beds ever since. Her instructor said to get fibre into the soil, suggesting they could throw in their old canvas shoes and carpets. My compost is always fibrous and chunky, partially undigested. My mother always said, "The proof of the pudding is in the eating," and my composts pass this test – my plants usually thrive beyond my expectations.

All my plans for doing the compost this winter have been squashed by this latest and most severe lower back problem. During the weeks of lying on my back I have done a lot of thinking and re-evaluating. It's been a good enforced rest from my busy ambitions, and a thoroughly painful and humbling experience.

Your description of the jewels of water on the arbutus leaves is so clear. I love finding those little round diamonds of water. One morning Ron and I were together admiring this year's most magnificent and wondrously huge nasturtium plant growing out of the sewer tile planter. One plant was so big and healthy that its many branches reached beyond the fence, into the wisteria and onto the path. It kept growing and growing and growing. On each large leaf was a jewel of water. Suddenly I thought of the Bushmen who live with so little water. They go around in their desert early in the morning, savouring these drinks left on plant leaves, one drop at a time. Ron and I did the same, tasting these tiny precious droplets, imagining without success how it would be to have only that for subsistence. Amazing, huh?

The most beautiful droplets coalesce on the leaves of the water lilies. Early morning sun on those droplets, rolling on the shiny, dark green

leaf surfaces, surrounded by lily flowers and pond water reflecting the sky and trees – these droplets win first prize for me.

∽

I brought one of the self-seeded nicotiana inside at the last possible moment before a hard frost. It continues to grow, bloom and release its fragrance each evening, extending our growing season for me. Summer is not over, the nicotiana are blooming. I've decided that next year I will dig up some of the volunteer plants and these will be my New Season's gifts – what wonderful offerings. Each evening when this plant sends its heady fragrance into the air of our early darkened December house, I get carried away. Such garden abundance could be overlooked because it is so easy.

Recently I watched a garden show (yes, on my back I surf the channels) and heard the host refer to my trifids as the "dreaded Himalayan balsam." Isn't that typical? Because they are easy-to-grow annuals which self-seed, they are denigrated and underrated. If they were hard to grow and had to be bought from a nursery, they would be considered a marvel. Bees covet these flowers, crawling inside them to get to the interior goodness. The fat bumblebees go inside the flowers and sometimes fall out the flower slits, looking quite clumsy until they realize they're heading for the ground. Soon the flowers are thoroughly dotted and frayed by the bees' entrances and exits. Later, the seed pods explode on touch, releasing a burst of seeds when you walk near them. What survivors those plants are. Four feet beneath our porch, in the almost dark, they pop up in the quarter-inch cracks between the cedar decking. I cannot but laugh at the sight. Too bad, my trifids, no prestigious awards for you: You are *too common*.

One summer I was at our local auction and there among the chairs, pictures, records, heaters, TVs and tupperware were five large black plastic pots of plants, each with one trifid. They were obviously grown in full sun and looking their best, but I gasped when they were auctioned off for $30 each. At home I had hundreds (thousands?) of them. I asked a person in the auction house, "Who is doing this and does it happen often?" She reluctantly told me that a small nursery regularly puts some in the auction and they always sell for between $15 and $35. She was personally horrified at "the deception" (as she called it), but there you go. They were intriguing enough to get sold for that much money.

⇜

December 3rd

I have been writing on the above for days, only able to sit upright for a few minutes at a time. Yesterday Ron helped me go see the bees. They are dead. The combs are empty; on the forest floor underneath, barely perceptible amongst the litter, are their bodies.

⇜

December 9th

I am not able to get to the computer very much now because of my back and other problems related to my injury. I have so much to talk about, but it will have to wait.

It is 22 degrees Fahrenheit now at 6:30 a.m. and I'm wondering what will happen to my roses, all bought last summer in memory of my mother. I have not mulched anything, nor has Ron had time to go outside. Well, this winter will be an acid test for my plants.

Love, Carol

WINTER

December 31st to January 6th

Dear Carol,

It is the last day of the year. Outside my window the witch hazel is blooming. It started about two weeks ago with an unmistakable red-orange tinge on the grey lichen-covered branches. I thought I was crazy. The strange flowers, not really flowers, more like clusters of curled fingers, never appear until well into January. I went out to check what was creating that fiery glow. It was the buds just beginning to burst their constraints. Now they are fully open. The February daphne too is starting to show a few lavender blooms. Both these shrubs have the sweetest scent in bloom. Since we are still likely to get a deep frost, it's hard to know whether to celebrate or fear for them.

I have been very conscious this autumn of the text of bare branches, a monochromatic interweaving like an Emily Dickinson poem. I kept collecting them for the house, wanting their Quaker simplicity rather than bought greenhouse flowers. The copper beech twigs still have their prickly nutshells hanging from them. The curled orange leaves still cling to the thorny berberis. On the way to a friend's house we passed a pile of yellow ochre willow shoots cut from a grove around a lake. We threw some in the back of the truck. At home I stuck some in the ground on the off chance they might root and took several bunches in the house.

These bony branches echo my desire to strip down to essentials, to go deeper into what I really want in my life, to get down to my own bones.

There is a bigleaf maple along the road where I walk most mornings. Weeks ago the leaves fell into fluffy piles, then slumped in the endless rain into a fabric that cloaked the earth like a patinaed silk shawl on an Edwardian piano. Finally in those very cold days, long white frost crystals etched the leaves, making them look softly furred and jagged all at the same time. I don't remember such dramatic frost crystals during other winters.

They stood up from the aged rings on the cedar fence posts like skyscrapers along city canyons. The clumps of couch grass took on architectural proportions, resembling metallic buttresses for tiny Gothic cathedrals. They rimed the single Oregon grape leaves at the end of each stem, barely touching the inner, more protected leaves, a litmus test of vulnerability.

This morning it is warm again. Just now I watched scores of tiny birds perched throughout the bare Japanese plum shifting ever so slightly, like leaves darkened by the season but still clinging to the branches. They took off and three sapphire-blue Steller's jays lighted in the small apple tree just outside this window. It's a convenient stop after scrounging for hazelnuts in the grove just beyond. I don't know if the nuts are empty or full – for the jays' sake I hope they found some good ones.

I have been hibernating these past weeks, doing almost nothing except reading, eating (trying not to have to cook) and sleeping. The holidays do that to me. On January second I feel ready to stretch a bit, released from this season of legislated emotion into a more ordinary freedom.

I was touched by your description of drinking the water drops on the trees. I do that too. Particularly I am inspired by the drops of water hanging off the hazelnut catkins when they first open. I always wonder whether the water will carry some almost subliminal floral essence. I sense it there — a faint perfume. Water has been so relentlessly present this fall that it is the ethereal fragrance that intrigues me rather than the water itself and the quirkiness of drinking like a passing deer.

The aconites are almost ready to burst. What a strange year this is.

Love, Dorothy

P.S. I was so sorry to hear of the death of your bees. Today, in this crazy chinook weather, the honeybees were out buzzing around the witch hazel, leaving their bright new year's splats as greeting cards on the car windshield.

CAROL'S JOURNAL

It drives me crazy to not be able to do even the simple things I used to do: typing, washing dishes, emptying the compost, small sewing projects, short walks, getting in the car and being driven places. When I think of my now-former life, before the recent back injury [later diagnosed as probably having been a ruptured disc], it seems like a fairy-tale life.

I've had two visits from the physiotherapist. She examined my back, showed me simple, easy stretches and told me to slowly, slowly increase what I do (what else is new?). The third visit was at 8 p.m. and the simple stretches she had me do left me in agony later in the night. I didn't know that it would be too much. She still doesn't understand how fragile CFS muscles are, but she is very sensitive and smart and will learn quickly. I still have to be helped to bathe because I can't carry the stool to the tub and can't bend over to pick anything up or bend to wash my legs below the knee.

We've adjusted to a new lifestyle and daily routine that fits my new body. It means Ron can't leave me alone for very long, and he does not make any evening or early morning appointments because of helping me with the bath things.

I am still not well enough to get in the car, drive to town, get out of the car and into a doctor's office, sit there waiting to be examined — they have no beds, only chairs or hard, high examining tables — and then go home again. Balancing what I would gain against the physical strain and energy drain, I simply can't do it.

January 23rd *Snow on the ground*

Dear Dorothy,

These past months have passed for me without nature's time markers. I feel so estranged from the natural world just outside my door. One day when the sun was shining and the deck was dry enough for me to walk on without fear of slipping, I saw one lone blue pansy blooming in the Chinese egg pot under the south-facing eaves. In my large strawberry planter next to the door was one valiant purple petunia. I know the petunia must live because of the heat that escapes from our front door; an R-2000 hermetically sealed house this is not.

The huge honeysuckle that has had leaf buds for a month or more appears to be trying to enter the house through the glass windowpanes. The branches next to the window have fully opened leaves. Just give it a break from this snow and cold and it will take off — always the first real

sign of spring. It grows against the cedar siding, nestled under the eaves, with roots and trunk protected under the decking. Now that we have had our big trees topped, it gets more winter sun.

⬎

I have been lying here rethinking the yard because it is painfully obvious that I will not be able to garden this year with any of my previous years' physicality. I will have to use my brain more and rely on others' bodies for brute work. I hope enough plants are established and enough routines in place so that Ron can carry on without my help. I have plans to have someone move my huge iris bed into raised planters, making them easier to keep weed free and separating them from the rock garden. Apart from that, I have no other plans. I will have to let flourish what will, relying on volunteers (both plants and workers).

In past years I have enjoyed starting some plants indoors, but this year will just sprinkle seeds on the warming spring ground. Who knows what I might find out by being restricted to doing less?

The Leylandi hedge looms darker, fuller and taller. Planted over five years ago as a natural-looking "fence" to mark our southern boundary, this hedge continues to rise, despite Ron's trimmings. It was Ron's first try at gardening, so he babied these weedy monsters and finds it hard to prune them seriously or regularly. He sees them as his wall against the encroaching world and seems unmoved by our original plan curtail them to the six-foot fence height.

When I first walked this two-acre property alone, the thing that sold me was the natural clearing, sun-drenched and hot: the field of my dreams. That summer there were thousands of Queen Anne's Lace blooming, along with a few feral and wild apple trees. This field incorporated about one-sixth of the two acres: I lay on my blanket in that field and said to myself, "This is home."

Now we have tamed that field. The great septic mound was put out there on the demand of the health department. With time and work it is now a lovely hill taking up two-thirds of the original field. The rest of the field is a mowed lawn we call the orchard, with more feral apples and clumps of everbearing raspberries. However, looming now along the whole south side of the orchard is the Leylandi hedge, reaching higher and higher. It shades almost the entire orchard all winter, creating a place of continual winter gloom. Where my field joined the Herb Farm field there is now a dark green wall. The Herb Farm reaps the benefits of our hedge, catching all the low winter rays, keeping the heat on their side.

I have talked with Ron about the shifting of the sun, the lack of air movement, the way the Leylandi winter-shadows the orchard, making the berry and apple roots experience an approaching ice age. I have shed tears as each winter I see the frostline of the hedge moving north. The hedge silently wins — barring the sun. It is as if nothing I say or do can express how it hurts my heart. I visually slash the branches to the ground daily, putting them through a shredder and freeing the field from their domination. Two years ago I explained how we could keep this hedge *and* have air movement and heat by cutting off its branches two feet above the ground. Not one branch was cut. In between times of real angst over the hedge I adapt an attitude of not caring. Maybe this will be a great experiment in how berries and apples fare in an arctic microclimate.

Now I have lost self-confidence. I am the trees in the shade, my roots

under the continually frost-heaved ground. As my unyielding body betrays me this winter, I look at the hedge and it is my enemy.

Ron's friend Judy, an artist in New Zealand wrote us this year about her latest artwork, her gallery shows and her angst over her work. I knew she was a gardener and she wrote a paragraph about it.

"Over the past five years I have been remaking our backyard. Most of it has been dug up and planted. My jungle has moments of great beauty when all the roses flower and moments of disaster when I clip and change and migrate my plants. This garden of mine is constantly changing. Very soon the jungle will be so intense that a map and guide will be required before one can venture into it. Jim was not amused at my taking over his yard, but he is now resigned to the jungle, which he asserts is what he had always planned for the area. But I have not done the job properly; I should have waited until the beds were correctly planned and prepared. Really now, do I have that much time to wait? It was and is my desire to enjoy this garden during my lifetime. Gardening is almost as much a challenge as painting. Ignorance is acceptable and all those pretty things have names some remembered, most not. Flowers don't need names to make them wonderful. My garden isn't clever because it's full of carefully selected and arranged plantings. It's a very pleasurable place because ignorance and happy accidents have become ideal helpmates in making this garden."

January 28th

It's night and I wondered why there was a glow outside. Full moon? I opened the door and saw the new white coating. Will this cold snap ever go? My stiffened back wants my legs to stride out full on the ground, and my senses long for the heady, earthy, mossy smells of our woods.

Love, Carol

February 2nd

Dear Carol,

I keep saying this winter is harder than any I remember, but then I think of one several years ago that was also icy cold, unremitting, with a real sense of the earth's death. I made a one-of-a-kind book that winter called "Desolation." The text was about ice and snow and cold and my associations with them. It comes to me clearly this winter that I don't really like the earth cloaked in snow, particularly on lead-sky days. The fir trees look black instead of green; the world seems drained of colours. There is no grey scale, no warmth or variation.

On Sunday it snowed again. I was invited to a wedding at the Sikh temple. The snow was thick; there was almost no visibility. We weren't sure about the roads but went anyway. At the temple I sat on the carpeted floor among women dressed in rich silks: magenta, clear red, emerald green, pink, ochre and lavender-grey. The bride was all red and gold. Through the window I could see the snow falling, but I felt warmed and revived by all that colour, as if I were in a June garden.

The next day the early sun was out clear and strong, casting a text of shadows on the snow: the almost square calligraphy of the wire fencing against the sparkling fields, and the stronger strokes of the tree trunks. I am in love with shadows, not for their tenebrous depths but because they speak of the sun lighting the world. It is on the desolate lead-sky days when there are no shadows that I feel the coldest.

Yet there are glorious moments. When the snow first fell I photographed the yellow catkins of the hazelnuts, all prematurely unfurled and now covered in snow. I photographed the fiery orange witch-hazel blooms wearing snowcaps. One night in our wood-heated hot tub I looked up at the dogwood tree and thought of New Year's celebrations in Japan. The round clumps of snow in the forked crooks of the branches looked just like the glutinous rice balls stuck on branches as propitious offerings for Japanese New Year.

The snow has been hard on the trees. Several large branches broke from one of our most graceful hawthorn trees and I had to free the hazelnut trees, which were all drooped and imprisoned. The hawthorn berries and the hazelnut flowers caught the snow and couldn't shake it off. I was struck by how well the evergreens are designed to hold the snow, then gently slide it away. In the woods I stood in snow caves formed under the cedar boughs. They would be perfect places to sleep, dry and insulated.

I walked again into the back woods yesterday, into a world of tracks and traces. There were deer tracks, snowed over, melted, retracked until they are all distorted — more expressionistic than journalistic. Through the gate to the pond the geese have tracked over and over their markings, giving the impression of a great migration on a goose highway. Everywhere on the crusted snow are tiny seeds of something, maybe Douglas fir — a random scattering, so very delicate. I felt as though something that had always been imperceptible was made visible. A gift.

Tomorrow is Tu B'Shevat, the New Year of the Trees. It is a minor

Jewish holiday that had its heyday among the mystics of the Middle Ages. There is a special meal at which four glasses of wine are drunk: the first pure white, the second white with drops of red, the third red with drops of white and the last pure red. During the meal a great range of fruits are eaten with each glass of wine: first fruits and nuts with hard outer cases, then fruits with hard inner pits, then fruits which can be eaten entirely and finally, with the red wine, only the essence of the fruitiest fruits is imagined. We will have a few friends over and tell tree stories. There is a Jewish saying: "If you are about to plant a tree and you hear the Messiah has come, first plant the tree, then go to greet the Messiah."

In preparation for telling my tree story, I visited the young pine that arrived magically maybe six or seven years ago. I think of this tree as an offshoot of the huge white pine that grew outside my childhood window. I remember climbing as high as I could on the branches of that other pine and jumping from its lowest branch into heaps of fall leaves we had piled underneath. That pine seemed haven and protection to me. This little pine is hope and continuity. A few clumps of snow were still clinging to its branches but mostly it had shaken itself free.

I have the seed catalogues stacked to remind me to get my orders together. A friend and I ordered some gourmet seeds from California. I didn't keep a record so now I can't remember what I still need. But really I am not one who loves to order seeds. I hate gardening in the cold, so I wait until the soil begins to warm and I can feel the sun on my back — then gardening feels like a restorative vacation on a tropical island. It's all a gamble anyway, since the hardier gardeners' peas often rot in the too-cold ground.

The aconites are all in bloom under the pear tree. Even when everything was covered with snow they somehow shed theirs and glowed like tiny suns. I wonder if they give off some inner heat.

I have such an image of your psychic war with your Leylandi hedge. Maybe you can cut strange shapes out of it: hearts and diamonds, birds and beasts, reverse topiary, poetic windows that will invite the sun back. Maybe you can gild the hedge so it gives off light and heat, creating an equatorial mini-zone. Maybe you can cut the tops off, leaving blunt supports for great tubs in which to grow twining vines that will interweave and dance with the Leylandi fronds. It must be getting late — I'm starting to hallucinate.

Take care, keep warm, drape rainbow scarves from your ceilings and dye all your underwear outlandish jewel tones. Fortunately, regardless of what we do or don't do, the days are getting longer and we will all some day soon feel the sun again with any luck, with any luck at all.

Love, Dorothy

CAROL'S JOURNAL

Cheryl, my physiotherapist, came again last week. She pronounced that my efforts are working. Mostly we talked about what I already do, and her advice is to just do more of the same few stretches and exercises before I tackle anything new. She is slowly starting to understand what CFS does to a person, but she still is thinking "normal" when she says, "If you do more exercise you will have more energy." I am so tired of educating the people who are supposedly caring for me. I could, if I had the energy, go through my mountains of articles on CFS and find the ones that talk about energy and exercise, but it would take so much out of me and I doubt she would read it. So I just listen to her and take from it what I can. Cheryl is surprised that no doctor is monitoring me with this injury, given my pre-existing health record, but I find that all younger, healthy people have unrealistic ideas of what doctors do.

No one knows what to do with me because there are no easy answers. No one knows what to do with any person with CFS other than to help them keep whatever physical mobility they have and encourage them to get lots of rest, live in quiet and peaceful surroundings, avoid all stress, etc. Even a "normal" person with the kind of spinal injury I have would not know what to do. In such cases, the current thinking is to exercise, maintain muscle tone and wait for nature to heal itself. Surgery often doesn't cure anything. I have to do exercises and stretching within my small limits because of CFS. I spend months working on physical progress another person might achieve in two days. For me, this is the only option, because I could not tolerate an operation.

Yesterday, ninety (90!) days since the day of my back injury, I got in to see my doctor. She said, "My, you are moving much better than I thought you would be." I said, "This is three months later and we have altered our lives around this injury and the physiotherapy to get me strong enough to be here. I couldn't come when I was worse." Really.

I was so overwrought from going to see her that I am still having repercussions this morning. I was upset about not being seen for so long and about her seeming non-involvement until I got well enough to come to her office.

She asked if I had a handicapped parking sticker and said she wanted me to have one. She filled out the form on the spot, and that was that. What a boost

this will be for us. When we go shopping Ron usually drops me off at the door, but I don't have my chair until he goes and parks and comes back with it. The first time we went to the mall in the ice and snow, he let me off at the door of Wal-Mart and I was so tipsy that a couple rushed to open the door and looked at me like I was drunk. Thank goodness my back strap was on and visible. I thanked them and said, "First time out since a terrible back injury." This is interesting: I always have to be sure that everyone knows I am "normal," I am good.

February 17th   *Rainy and mild*

Dear Dorothy,

The days and nights this past week, so springlike and warm, washed away almost all memory of the weather weirdness we endured before. Arctic one week, spring the next. That is the miracle of our coast. I have started to feel like I am over another invisible hump. With physiotherapy of my own making (the pool and a walk, stretches and constant monitoring of my back) the horror of the preceding three months is fading. All these changes for the good happened within days of each other, and during the cutting of the Leylandi hedge.

Since writing you last, I again campaigned to have the hedge cut to the originally agreed-upon six-foot height. Again I encountered the same non-compliance — a passive resistance that still leaves me baffled. Ron did trim the hedge, not adhering to either form or function but to his own set of inner struggles with the world. It looked like one of the Three Stooges' haircuts. I used more persuasion, common sense and what I thought was flawless logic. The hedge was destined to loom, so when all my big guns had been used, I pulled out my secret weapon, my last letter to you. Ron laughed and I cried. He said, "You can write. You could make Hitler cry." By the time I finished my noon sleep, the hedge was almost done — massive cuts, stems like small trees on the ground.

I thought I would be happy, and I was satisfied, but victory it was not. On the third day of our very warm weather, I walked in bright sunlight in the area formerly shadowed by the hedge, and the frost heaves were still there, my feet crunching on ice. Why could I not have prevailed before? I think the hedge echoed too closely dark parts of my own past.

Like you, Dorothy, I have never been a seed catalogue enthusiast. I don't think I knew they existed before I immigrated to Canada. My first and last brush with them was on moving to Briarwood. I ordered some privet hedges (along with other plants) because I had read how wonderful they were, and how fast they grow. What finally arrived in June from an Ontario company was a joke. I think the self-bonsaied bodies of those original privets still live on at Briarwood, now a three- or four-foot scraggly mess. I know my ignorance was to blame: I ordered things from an eastern company without thinking about our climate or the needs of the plants I ordered. And I believed those enticing colour photographs and was lured by the offer of so many "free" bulbs. Oh, and the precious asparagus they sent: a dozen plants, tiny seedlings, wizened and dry and doomed to be stunted from then on. A few years later I planted my own asparagus seeds — over 300 — and they grew like the weeds they are. In fact later I found that you can seed asparagus at ground level, like most

other plants — no warfare-sized trenches are necessary. Once established they seed themselves, the volunteer plants making wonderful gifts for friends who think growing asparagus is difficult.

⟿

Since the sun came out and the hedge went down and my body became a little more limber, I have revised my garden plans. I will grow only those things that require no work except watering. I will plant anything that sounds interesting. I will ask for a seed or two from my gardener friends' packets, just to try in a pot on the deck or in an existing bed. I have already experimented with poking a long stick in the ground. I *can* do that. I will make a map of the cultivated part of our yard and mark each of the seeds I place.

Ron has wholeheartedly agreed to make a bed on wheels for me to use in the yard. I have wanted this for a few years but made do with a lounge chair. Now I will have a sort of wheelbarrow version of a bed, with an attachment in which to place a garden umbrella, my reading material, drawing pads, writing material and a cup of tea. I picture myself a lady of leisure, wearing a wild garden hat, armed with a poking stick and an eagle eye, overseeing the yard and the birds. Maybe I will cover the umbrella and my hat with fronds and the birds will think I am a bush.

This is the year I will wear purple and outlandish outfits. (The neighbour's children already think I do.) I've dyed everything I wear with the limited selection of bright colours from cheap dye packets bought at the grocery store: purple, blue, burgundy and green. (I'm not a fan of yellow or orange.) I use "lady gloves" from the Salvation Army for gardening, and they will hit the dye pot too. If I cannot grow as many flowers this year, I will dress in my favourite flower colours. Maybe this is my preparation for becoming a grandmother. This coming child will know me as the "purple lady with the outdoor bed on wheels." I could think of worse things. Makes me wonder what my own round, grey granny was like before I came upon the scene.

Ron has spotted many bright orange goldfish in the pond, the babies that survived last year's many attacks by the great blue heron. Now they are big, bright and visible. Gads, if only they would stay a brownish colour and remain hidden from the heron. They grew and thrived despite the constant run-off from the new ditch in the orchard — surviving against all that the pond books recommend.

The honeysuckles are leafing out and becoming the first significant spring green in the yard. Meanwhile we still have the heady fragrance every night from the nicotiana brought to the windowsill last fall. With stems many feet long lying in amongst the leaves of the large jade trees, they survive and give nightly pleasure. They keep alive the hope of spring and the fragrances of honeysuckle, lilac, wisteria, lily-of-the-valley and iris.

Next sunny warm morning I may have the heart to walk to see the beehive. One friend suggests that a small nucleus of bees might have lived and will emerge on a warm day. Such an upbeat person. I am fearful to find out. Maybe I will never go back, and assume they are fine.

Love, Carol

March 1st

Dear Carol,

I am reeling and disoriented. The pink buds on the Japanese plum branches forced in the dining room cry out that the season will change, is changing, but only a few days ago I was nibbling off the icy casings that outlined each twig of the dormant roses and melting their crackly coldness in my mouth. It swings between tropical and arctic and I lie low, waiting for a steadier siting of the season. This is the red season: The naked trees that should look dull in their barrenness glow. Is their blood rising in readiness, or is the glow from angry frustration at being so cold for so long?

The farm geese shriek in the night, standing in an unruly flock under the barn light. It's mating season. Last week they walked about as if they were in some high-school yard, the ganders carefully shepherding their chosen females, the females turning their beaks down demurely. I thought of sewing them letter jackets so they could really look the part. Things are rawer this week. The mating pairs do a dance in any available puddle, a sinuous snaking of their necks, then the gander mounts, then another gander, trying to make sure only he fathers anything, grabs the mating gander by the wing and drags him off. The dog goes nuts.

Last week on my usual walk I saw the wind had torn clumps of lichen out of the trees. It is *Evernia prunastri*, one of the two local lichens that ferments in ammonia to make a fuchsia dye. I gathered up the clumps thinking I might try it on paper fibre. Crouching low to get them, I saw the newest young nettle shoots just emerging from the soil — almost time for nettle soup and nettle pancakes.

And yet only a day or so later I saw the snowdrops totally encased in

ice, looking like anti-lanterns in a fairy tale about the Ice Kingdom. These contrasts put me on a rack of confusion, alternately having the confidence to open to a warmer, gentler world and then scuttling back to lean against the wood stove. The sun is so warm and bright and encouraging in the middle of the day, but the chicken coop roof is still patchy and white, and in sheltered patches along the driveway there are mounds of snow. So, now you know: I am only a fair-weather friend and I rail against the tenacity of this winter kingdom.

Congratulations on the taming of the hedge. Since I started writing this, very early in the dim morning light, the sun has come up strong and is melting away my aggravation. As ever there is too much to do, too little time. The four guinea fowl graze peaceably in front of my studio like slow-moving rocks, only a raised red-topped head every so often gives them away.

Love to you, Dorothy

March 19th

Dear Dorothy,

This winter has been too long and too sad. My depressed and reflective mood is caused by a combination of things: my back injury and subsequent major physical restrictions; the unrelenting cold weather; and the recent loss or serious illness of so many close female relatives and friends.

This hard, cold winter followed now by a reluctant spring has me reeling with memories. So many plants in my yard hold memories of people who gave them to me or for whom they are named: Ruth's lilac, Nora, Evie, a water lily now divided into three, called the Three Faces of Eve, Mary, Dorothy, the Three Sisters, Frederick, Ulysses. Some are named for animals and places: the Goat Apple, the Horse Apple, the Bird Window, Bee Tree, the Haul Road Apple, Bird Bush. As I pass by each plant I chant its history: "You came from the old homestead site on the Malahat – you are the descendants of our pioneers from one hundred years ago"; "You are the plant Aaron bought for Ron's birthday and you are the plants Ron got for Father's Day"; and "You are the plants we rescued when the bulldozers came through Mill Bay." Although people leave our lives, plants remain as living testament to the continuity of life, each year renewing with hope and helping us relive our own history.

These thoughts bring up earlier memories to do with plants. When I was a child of eleven, my family moved back to Springfield, Illinois, from Centralia. We lived in a rented duplex on the outskirts of town, with a large, mysterious wilderness almost bordering the house. There was a huge hollow filled with trees, and all around the edges were trees draped with vines. Some of the vines were so long they doubled back from the treetops and hung, as if waiting for me. They were plenty strong enough for us to swing on, and we did, jumping out over the cliff like Tarzan. Nestled in the centre of these wilds was a small structure in perpetual shadow, surrounded almost completely by a tangle of growth. A witch was said to live there, and although I never saw her, I was sufficiently frightened by the stories that I kept my distance.

On high ground at the edge of the tree-filled hollow was a cluster of

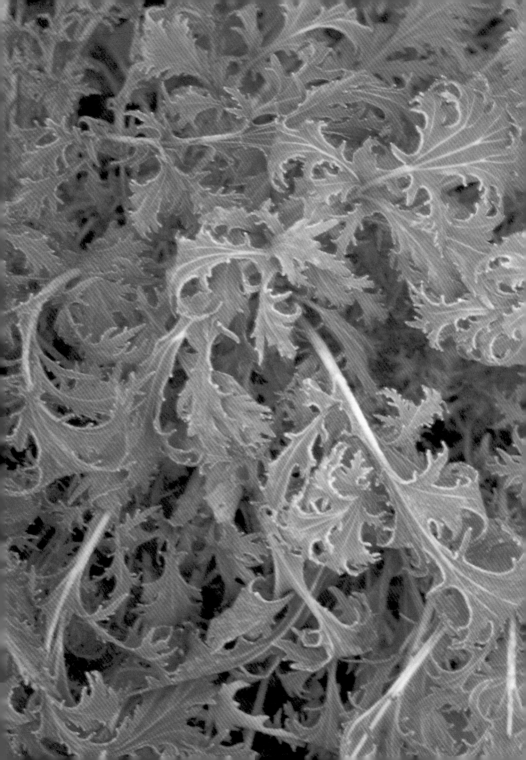

the most wonderful flowers: the size of ordinary violets and with the coloration of pansies. I, the lone explorer/botanist, named them pansy-violets, a name that sticks with me to this day. I was captivated by these plants, so foreign to me and so forbidden by their location. As I was never sure if the witch cultivated them, I always approached them nervously, "thinning" them bit by bit. Next to our sterile new duplex I piled rocks and soil and planted pansy-violets. I next saw pansy-violets over thirty years later, on this island. They are the common Johnny-jump-ups and grow here like weeds. My heart started that almost painful thudding when I saw them again. I still look at them with special vision and am again swinging on the vines.

From that rented house we moved to a house my parents bought, a bald four-room box that squatted perilously close to a four-lane high-way. What I remember most vividly are the early morning walks I took with my mother down to a little stream, crossed by the highway. At the edge of the creek was a bush where masses of violets grew. I can never see a violet without thinking of my mother and those walks and our long, private talks, which were very important to me then. Now, almost a half century later, I live on these two acres with wild violets in so many colours — fragrant ones in purple, pink, white and even slightly striped mutants, and the unscented yellow ones, which bloom after the purples. Every year after Mother's stroke I picked bouquets of them for her. I was then the keeper of those violet memories, hers having been stolen in that split-second silent burst of one blood vessel.

⤚

In going through yet another box of old photos, a small black-and-white Brownie photo of my cactus garden leapt out at me. It was 1957 or 1958, and we lived in El Centro, California, a border town locally called the "hellhole of the U.S." because it's situated well below sea level and has unbelievable summer heat and humidity. In the small plot of land next to the trailer where we lived, I dug a round garden and transplanted one of every kind of cactus I liked from the surrounding desert country. I brought the sand back from the desert and surrounded the plot with rocks. The summer before I gave birth to my first son, I had to leave because the heat made me so ill. Upon returning from Illinois, I found that my husband had "watched the garden," meaning he had watered it frequently. My cacti were rotted.

I have a photo of Mother in her wheelchair, here on my deck, reaching down to dead-head the petunias in a container. She told me, "They will grow more if you prevent them from going to seed." Interesting that we use that phrase negatively, to describe a woman past her youth. Yet in going to seed, each plant holds all the genetic memory and is ready to renew again – older women have so much experience and wisdom.

Ron is transplanting and weeding the iris. He just came in and said, "Does this make your heart happy?" My throat constricts with emotion knowing that he is doing this for me. I remember how many places these irises came from and how lovingly I have cared for them. I can still say to them: "You came from Suzanne's yard the year I helped her thin her irises"; "You came from thinnings at the Mill Bay Centre"; "You came from the ditch along Cobble Hill Road." They are not just a variety pack from the nursery. Each plant has a story, and it is my story.

Love, Carol

SPRING

March 27th

Dear Carol,

I was so touched by your letter and your thoughts of friends. I noticed a day or so ago that the dogwood we planted for Rudy's mother when she died has blooms formed and ready. It is a Korean dogwood with small starry flowers borne on a fragile network of twigs. This will be its second season of bloom. It feels right that it should project such effortless physicality, such lightness – a kind of gift and reparation for the many years Nelly struggled with crippling arthritis.

When I first met Nelly she was still in the big Berkeley house with a wonderful yard out back where she puttered around. Later, when she couldn't manage the big house, she moved to an apartment overlooking San Francisco Bay. She had a balcony but it was so cold and windswept that nothing would grow. She missed being rooted, walking out her door and stepping into a garden where things grew.

I am as ever struck by your childhood gardening stories. Though my mother gardened during the years I was growing up, I took very little interest. I remember her telling me she thought some day I would enjoy gardening and she was right, though I am such a haphazard sort of gardener. When Cicely was a toddler I used to lure her into the vegetable garden where I was weeding the rows of new seedlings. She had a wonderful book called *Shrewbettina's Birthday* and I'd tell her I'd just seen Shrewbettina hiding under some leaves. It worked for a while but she soon figured out the truth. In the perennial bed she'd collect worms in a yellow plastic pail, naming the mother, father and babies. That kept her occupied for a while. Later I ordered special variety packs of seeds for kids, mixed flowers, mixed radishes. We bought her the most beautiful Smith and Hawken child-sized rake. Nothing really held her interest. She would rather lie in the hammock, with or without a book, any day. In July of course she was happy to raid the pea patch, but other than that and when I'd send her to get me some parsley or chives for dinner she's managed to avoid the garden. I tell myself she'll enjoy gardening when she's older. It seems important to me, this generational connection.

Rudy's sister Letty has a house in Pinole where there is endless sun. We bought her a few fruit trees when she first moved in, but somehow she was not that enthused about them. At some point she began to go to rose shows and at the end of the day she could buy the rose cuttings for a few cents. She stuck them in the ground and now she has a jungle of thorny bushes covered with huge blooms in every possible colour. They aren't the old-fashioned roses that I am mad for, but I love the wild abandon, the total lack of garden scheme, the outrageous energy of those bushes. I don't think she prunes them or does anything much to them, but in California they just grow.

These nights are still crisp and with luck the mornings crystalline. It is magnolia time. This spring I've been stroking the magnolia buds – the great swollen ones on the *magnolia soulangiana* and the small compact ones on the *magnolia stellata*. They are all grey with a gentle fuzz like a sweet sleek cat. I thought they might be slightly bristly or abrasive but they are velvety. Now as the days warm, the deep rosy purple of the *soulangiana* begins to expose itself, just slivers at a time. Their modesty reminds me of a bather, testing the lake water with her toes, slowly letting her robe slip from her shoulders but still protective. I am waiting for that moment when the sun warms enough that one by one they throw caution to the wind and unfurl their luscious flesh. It's not safe though, really. If the temperature drops fast, they are often frozen into shrivelled defeat. It is a gambling time, this early spring, and with all my heart I wish them the best.

This past weekend Rudy and I accomplished in no time at all a job I thought would be huge and onerous. We dug out the plants in the boxes between the house and the sheds. Years ago Rudy filled the boxes when I wasn't paying attention with the most dreadful soil, which he masked with some ok stuff on top. For years everything I planted became instant bonsai. You'd think I might have done something sooner, but I am good at procrastinating and as the time went by the job seemed more and more impossible.

My idea is that the boxes will be mainly santolina which looks good most of the year. I have made cuttings and they are starting to come along. I replanted them with a few primula and the bulbs that were already in the box. I transplanted the hollyhocks out by the red shed where they will be happier or disappear. I will miss their height and the way they cast shadows on the green shed wall but I will not miss their pocky drooping leaves. They do not seem to thrive in boxes. I banished the ravenously spreading marguerite daisies to the fence by some roses. In the boxes they looked alright for about ten minutes. Out in the grass if they survive they will make me happy; if not, that's ok too.

Last fall I hired a guy to help me with my other nightmare – the perennial border. My back is too touchy. If I kneel to weed for too long I can't stand up again. I used to discipline myself to weed only a section at a time but by the time I got through once, the whole thing needed weeding again. The guy cleared out most of the weeds and assorted oddments. What's left now is mostly my favourites – the peonies, Siberian irises and day lilies. Rudy and I stopped off at a nursery that specializes in native plants. I interplanted the perennials with red osier, dogwood, Indian plum and ocean spray. They should be fairly carefree once they're established and pretty easy on water during the summer drought. At the moment it looks promising but that is the way with new plantings. I imagine soon more of the most horrible weeds, dandelion (which I love to eat in spring and even love the look of the flowers, but which are awful in a bed), buttercup (which is awful anywhere) and burdock (with a root that goes straight to hell), will turn up. Then if the new shrubs get happy, they will probably go wild and make a thicket that I will have to hack back to get even glimpses of the peonies, but as I say, there is nothing but hope in a neat new planting and I am happy.

I like the gardening this time of year. I like clipping away deadwood and the remains of last year's growth that I should have trimmed in the fall and didn't. I like seeing the new buds just about ready to pop. The Japanese plums and the almond are blooming now, delicate pale pink. A blooming almond tree is as close to a vision of paradise as I can imagine. The peaches are starting. The cherries are almost ready to burst. This morning from the window I watched a drake open his scissor beak and squawk three times with metronome precision. With each squawk a gentle breath of very unmechanical mist emerged to float on the morning stillness.

This gardening is an endless reality check. I have no end to vision and a limited amount of perseverance to make it happen. Oh for staff. The daffodils I planted last fall between the *rosa rugosas* along the driveway are up – dozens of King Alfreds. Boring but serviceable. Meanwhile the lovely mixed ones that I've planted over the years around the terrace and between the black currants have reduced themselves to a few reedy leaves and no blooms. Not planted deep enough? Not enough fertilizer? Some invisible below-ground attacker? By now, in my vision, they were to have naturalized into drifting yellow and white clouds. If I have learned anything it is not to be too invested in my vision, to have many mini-visions, to wait and see where my vision will mesh with the earth's own inclinations, to take great pleasure in the fleeting successful moments.

Last fall I moved a magical yellow peony from the dreaded perennial border. It bloomed weeks before anything else, a lone light in an otherwise desolate garden. I moved it by the back door where I have other things that start in the bleakness of winter's end. The leaves are a very dusty purple that is perfect with the pink blossoms of the February daphne and wonderful with the miniature yellow narcissus that have been up for the last three weeks. Now wonder of wonders I see the peony will actually bloom this spring. The rich round buds are visible as the leaves begin to stretch and loosen. This peony came from an old friend, Peg, who also gave us the miraculous unnamed grapes. Gardens are such a mnemonic mosaic, any detail having the possibility of triggering layered associations to people and moments past, so much remembering. Like Proust's madeleines.

Your letter and the pale grey of today, after several clear blue ones, leave me with a feeling of melancholy. It is such a trick, being alive to oneself and the earth. I am grateful as I notice the scilla and violets spreading blue and purple through the grass in yearly widening circles that I am surrounded by growing things rather than concrete towers. It seems a better arena to learn something of this crazy Kali cycle of creation yielding to destruction and opening again into creation.

Love, Dorothy

CAROL'S JOURNAL

I have been in the doldrums of feelings from this "back thing." It seems to me that apart from the recent injury, I have something chronic that never returns to normal. I cannot regain agility because my lower back gets fatigued so easily that it is imperative that I lie down. Off and on I continue to have sensations of slight numbness/electricity/burning in my right foot, especially in the big toe and the toe next to it. Sometimes it spreads here and there, now even to my left calf.

The trip to the back specialist on Thursday was one of the most arduous things I have done. He did adjustments to correct the twist in my spine, and my body was jerked quite a bit. It did release my back so that I could reach much further to my toes, but at what price? Five days later the extension I had immediately after the adjustment is gone because I was so sore and stiff from the muscle overuse during the procedure.

The day after that appointment I had a complete physical drop. It was very scary, very much like the old CFS *that I control now. The trip, the treatment, the heat, the conversation, the fear and mistrust I feel whenever I don't connect with the person who is treating me: all of it brought me down very, very hard. Plus I didn't have time to ask all the questions I needed to about aftercare, exercises, prevention, etc. Ron and I have decided to wait until the week after this to give me a chance to work up enough strength to handle another visit.*

⪡

I'm on the couch with the small new keyboard on my lap, the newish big screen on a rolling cart, along with my notebook computer and a bag of bricks to counterbalance the whole affair. All very "high tech," har, har. I am working on the next of the gardening letters to Dorothy. I am one letter behind, because of the back / leg / foot numbing which makes me not able to work on the computer in a comfortable way. Today we are fine-tuning the whole thing to work in three ways: sitting on a chair, sitting in my La-Z-Boy chair, and lying on this couch with upper torso slightly raised and a pillow under my head. All of these ways require my body to make adjustments and require muscles that have to be developed slowly. Sitting regularly produces a variety of foot problems, from numbing toes to tingling, from total numbness and coldness to burning sensations, all of which tend to curtail the creative juices I can attest to.

April 9th   *A spring afternoon*

Dear Dorothy,

Here I am, lying down with my latest computer set-up. This means learning new body positions with a small keyboard on my stomach, a real test of my touch-typing. If I can get this to work for me, my options are greatly increased.

In this cold wet spring I have been limited by my body to observing nature. No clipping or weed pulling. My choices are either to give up or find ways to manage with this latest physical limitation. I looked each day for signs of our three trilliums, and *voilà*, they finally appeared. Fallen tree branches from the many storms had crushed one of them, so it grew and bloomed horizontally. How could I help but be moved by its predicament? In the next day or two I asked Ron to uncover it and look more closely. It is not exactly a trillium. I dub it duallium: two full leaves and one residual; two flower petals, but three sepals. This plant is not "normal" and is more interesting for its deviations. Two of our single trilliums have double blooms this year – natural changes, it seems.

Your description of the magnolia made me smile and think of the many times I've stroked the limbs of arbutus. Is there anything more delightful than running your hands up and down and around a limb of that marvellous tree, into the crevices, wrinkles and twists of its form? It is hauntingly familiar to my touch. One of my simple pleasures is using a small cascara tree that grows just off our deck as a walking support – a vertical handrail. Each day as I walk to the pool, I swing around on it, the feel of its bark so pleasurable as it steadies me. When I began doing this five years ago, I could put my hand completely around it; now two hands are needed to encircle it. Certainly I would have missed its steady growth without this accidental marker.

As this cold spring moves on I keep changing my expectations of the garden and myself. In years past I mentally "saved" the front field for the future, thinking that someday a grown child of ours would want to grow a market garden there. The soil is so fertile, its location to the sun is fairly good, water is plentiful and there is easy access to the road. But this past winter I realized that none of our children share my interests. I am learning all over again that our children are not ours, and that my special sight is *mine*. The front field is now the domain of all things wild: birds, cats, blackberries, feral apples and alder, with a backdrop of a giant ancient arbutus, Ulysses, its trunk more than thirteen feet in circumference. My fantasy now includes cow parsnips and teasel standing high above the blackberries, transforming the field into my secret place.

In my wanderings over these acres this spring I see how the violets are taking over and your sweet cicely is moving into places it likes. Waxberry bushes are coming in where they were not before and three kinds of wild roses line the side of the drive. It makes me think again that this is the way of my future: Observe everything that is already here, continuing to toss seeds and see what likes to grow. I need not "improve" it endlessly. Being busy always gets in the way of observation. My seventh year here is ending: It's a time for standing still.

Love, Carol

April 13th
Dear Carol,
Well, the nights have been too cool. The magnolias, so potent in their potential, are all black and shrivelled. How many lessons do I need about

enjoying the moment for itself, dousing expectations? If you meet the Buddha on the road, kill him. I've never understood what that meant but it seems relevant. The rains are relentless – the newly popped narcissuses are prostrate, their heads touching the ground. Oh, spring, I entice you, I entreat you, oh, spring.

⤚

I have been thinking how much I love this season, which is so much about potential. It is "the season of dots." When the white plum blossoms first appear they are like disembodied sphericals strung along the branches. Gradually they open, but still the blossoms at the farthest ends are just dots. I love this time of definition better than when the tree is in full glorious flower. I like the feeling of introspection, the quietness of self-knowledge. The plum tree always blooms before the leaves come out. The pink colour of the Japanese plum blossoms is so heavenly I used to hate it when the bronzy red leaves began to appear, giving the tree a rusty look. Now I have come to like that turning time when the pink has a metallic tinge, the moment after perfection. It reminds me of *The Book of Tea*, which describes the beauty of leaves scattered on a stone path, and also of *The Tale of Genji*, which rhapsodizes the petals of flowers past their prime. I find now that I like the moments before and after perfection better than perfection itself.

There are lots of dots these days – like a Morse code world of dots and dashes. Along the road is a shrub I've never noticed before, one with tiny red dots of new leaves along slender grey stems. The hawthorns are green dots on tan branches. There are also white dots against ruddy brown stems and silver on grey. The lilacs are different – not spheres but miniature wheat sheaves, the layered leaves barely shielding the tightly furled lavender buds inside.

Right now the farm is strewn with my prunings. In my haphazard way I walk around with my clippers, cutting deadwood, allowing the vitality of the form to emerge from the shadowing of last year's dried blooms, discoloured stems and criss-crossed branches. I let the clippings fall on the grass and keep moving, planning of course to come back through with the big garden cart. Rudy hates it. At the moment the heaps are so big that I really will have to clean them up soon. It's beginning to bug even me.

∿

I wanted to tell you my story about comfrey. When we first bought the farm there was a big holly tree outside what is now our bedroom, and beside it a patch of comfrey. I had read about all the wonderful qualities of comfrey, how you could feed a whole flock of sheep or goats on almost nothing, how you could fix broken bones and stop bleeding, etc. Regardless, I didn't want the comfrey there and tried to dig it out. As many times as I did, it always came back. Finally we cut down the holly tree. It blocked too much light and I was tired of stepping barefoot onto the skeletal holly prickles that looked benign but bit deep. I guess we disturbed the soil enough so that the comfrey finally gave up. Still, after it was gone I missed the strange tubular comfrey flowers hanging in graceful arcs.

I decided two springs ago to plant some comfrey in front of my studio. It didn't seem happy and it disappeared. Yesterday I noticed two tiny new comfrey leaves poking up where I had thought it was gone. This makes me think of the plant world as a consciousness that can go underground and remain dormant, at least to our perceptions – a fermenting silence, a hibernation. If I put my ear to the ground, could I move beyond my usual thresholds to hear the vegetative forces dreaming? And would that help me stay deeper in tune with my own inner dreaming, what I call "the intimate unknown?" And is it perhaps these tenuous connections to the mysteries of life force itself that make both wild and cultivated gardens such rich humus, such a throbbing labyrinth path to the unknown?

I often fall into despair when plants seem to abandon me. Sometimes I read disaster too soon. Last summer I planted a strange ghostly monks-hood, white with secret blue inside. I've had a deep blue-black one for years and loved its brooding presence. In some perverse way I also loved knowing it is very poisonous. The new white one sickened and shrivelled, making me wonder if there was something wrong with the soil there. This spring I see a mound of monkshood leaves where I thought it was gone for good. Maybe this is a lesson for me about withholding judgments around people, too. To wait, not losing faith. Maybe people, like plants, move in and out of harmony, coming around in their own season.

We used to have one trillium growing by the holly tree, just one transplanted from the woods. It never spread but every year it appeared, a signpost, a reminder that out in the back woods there were hundreds of trilliums waiting for a visit. When we took out the holly, the trillium left too. I miss that spring reminder to go into the woods. That one trillium, first in pointy bud, then with a pure white triangle of petals un-furled and finally gone pink, was a sign like the first swallows returning.

As I write of trilliums, I think of a property down the road. There used to be a triangle of woods, mostly Douglas fir, which in spring sup-ported the thickest growth of trilliums I've ever seen. Someone bought

the place, logged the woods and resold it. I don't care about the obscene profit they made but I still mourn the sacrifice of the trilliums. Lately as I've walked along the road I've seen five or six trilliums hiding in the grass, the only survivors of that terrible decimation.

This is such a deceptive time of year. The damp grey seems unchanged from the blanket of immobility that marks the winter months, except warmer. But in fact the world is changing at lightning speed and if I am not alert I miss whole acts in a vibrant drama. The rock maples had minute scarlet excrescences only a few days ago. I wanted to photograph them but didn't get around to it. They have passed through two or three new stages since then. The cherry seems to have moved from being in bud to being almost at peak while I turned my back. It challenges me to stay awake. The black currants have the tiniest blossoms still in bud, an unearthly delicate bluish-purple lit with green. One old traditionalist hen has defied modern engineering and hatched a batch of chicks. They stay sheltered under her or sit on her back. They too are dots, but only for a short time. Soon they will be gangly teenagers with punk feathers half grown out and then by summer they will be modest young matrons and strutting cocks.

Best to you, Dorothy

April 16th *Another cold day*

Dear Dorothy,

I did love your comfrey story. I could tell a similar one from my early days at Briarwood. I tried to eat comfrey years ago, and once treated an abscess with it, which didn't work. However later on it proved to be one of the most successful plants to press into clay. It decorated hundreds of my plates, platters and baking dishes. The fine hairs on the back side of its leaves left impressions in the clay that picked up the staining perfectly after the first firing.

In the second half of my pottery career I began to find ways to use plants in the pottery. By the time I had to give up making pots, about one-third of my pots had plant impressions, mostly wild plants. I always wrote the name of the weed onto the back of the pot and felt I raised plant appreciation in this way. Almost everyone who bought my pottery was amazed that they loved the weed-covered pots. Queen Anne's lace, dillweed, comfrey, self-heal, parsnip, fireweed, ferns, shepherd's purse – if I could press it and get a stain to stay, I did. One summer afternoon, a party of customers from the Prairies found their way to my showroom. When I went to see how they were doing, I received a chewing-out that was so unexpected it left me speechless. The angry, red-faced man, a Saskatchewan farmer, thought it blasphemous to glorify weeds. He was genuinely outraged.

Your story of the destroyed trillium patch made me think about the ways we relate to plants. Our collective thinking is changing, as we become painfully aware that our treatment of earth's plant life is going to bring us to our knees. "Hug a Tree" and "Save a Rainforest" are slogans, but they hold our future. Forests full of plants are disappearing before we even know what they contain, and we could be the next endangered species without them.

The first plant I fell in love with, over twenty-five years ago, was the teasel. After years of finding it, growing it, studying it, selling it, drawing it and using it as my logo on business cards and stationery, I can say I am a bit dotty over teasel. When I find them anywhere it is like seeing family. I sold some teasel seed to the nursery at the Roadside Pantry years ago, and now they grow in little stands here and there. They are my kin. I feel all warm and proprietorial about them.

The teasel that now grows in my yard is descended from the first ones I dug out of a farmyard in Fulford Valley, Saltspring Island, twenty-nine years ago. I sprinkled my teasel seed in the ditch on Saltspring, where my friend Ingrid died, to honour her memory. I gave pots of it to my friend Beryl when they left on a barge for a summer home on the south side of Provost Island. She planted them around the outhouse there, and they thrived for the ten summers Beryl's family stayed there.

As you well know, my most fatal attraction was with cow parsnip. I screamed with delight and disbelief when I first saw them growing along the railroad track in Parksville. Twelve feet tall, majestic, they glowed gold in their end-of-summer drying stage. After I established them in my own yard, I gave friends dried seed heads, eighteen inches across, extolling their virtues. I remember Rudy digging out some roots for me from your place, shaking his head with disbelief. My love affair ended when I found out, the hard way, that they can produce a skin rash and itch of life-altering proportions. But there are photos of summer days past, with me nestling in their giant leaves or standing on a ladder, encircling the top flower head with my arms – like something from a science fiction movie set.

Dorothy, I wanted to tell you about Ron's pond. Remember last year he drained the orchard with proper trenches, gravel, drain pipe – the whole thing? Draining that bog that was caused by the natural lay of the land and the neighbours' failing septic system was a good thing – but he seemed to lose his vision. He ended the pipe at his pond, which he had lovingly dug by hand two years before, creating a wonderful spot for plants and fish. I pointed out that the draining waters would be bad for the pond, would jeopardize its health. The books all said, "No"; logic said "No." Like with the Leylandi hedge, I was at a loss as to why he did what he did. But in a new state of equanimity I said to myself, "Let happen what will happen."

And it did. The evil waters carried silt, septic nutrients and mysterious unknowns into the pond, disrupting the delicate balance it had attained. All winter the pond looked murky, with grey-buff streams swirling in it. During the first warmish days it took on the look of a cesspool. I recognized the colour and knew that sudden death was imminent. For all the equanimity I had achieved, I nagged and pleaded for the pond, being its advocate, calling for emergency action. Ron talked about his timetable, including a complete renovation of the system in the summer. I mentally rolled my eyes heavenward. However, a day or two later he was in the pond, routing the drain through it and to the other side. The water is now streaming out on the lower side of the pond and into the back forty and beyond. I'm not sure whether this can overcome the damage and ever-increasing algae blooms. The fish still live, but no frogs have come. Last year our frog population had increased to eight.

The water plants look very sick. Hard to tell what they will do because the spring is so slow. The sight of Ron, up to his thighs in the cold pond, working in the muck, was almost too much. I wanted to cry and I wanted to laugh. He ran clear well water for a day or two. From our top deck I watch him: like a sea farmer harvesting kelp, he rakes and scoops the algae daily.

Being the opportunistic gardener I am, I am using the masses of algae in the compost and directly on the plants themselves. Who knows what magical component it has. Well, *he* is using the algae on the plants. I am still behind the scenes, the tape falling off my mouth often.

Love, Carol

CAROL'S JOURNAL

My new method of setting up the computer is working very successfully. I do get some eyestrain, but with practice as to distance, brightness and so on, this will lessen. With not sitting so much, my leg problems are less and my spirits much higher.

I've seen a foot specialist and then had another appointment with the back specialist. He sincerely believes that my problems are due to an irritated sheath of the spinal cord and nerve leads to my leg, which cannot clear of toxins fast enough. This sounds so familiar to me because CFS is very slow recovery from activity. Fatigue comes because your body does not clear ordinary toxins. We really do not appreciate how much the body constantly repairs itself and gets rid of waste products from energy expended until it stops doing it efficiently. Until then we take it all for granted.

Whenever I make appointments with health professionals I have to go at my best time, not only because it is the only time I can do it, but also because I need to look good. Good enough not to be written off. I make sure that I'm dressed nicely, even put on a bit of make-up. I try to look like someone worth saving or paying attention to. I go when I don't slur my speech. I do it when I can be my old self mentally, ask the right questions, for my own sake, and so the medical person will do his/her best for me. My little life is spent trying to have contact with the outside world and trying to find ways to not freak doctors out and send them away. Ron says he can smell the fear in doctors when they see something they can't explain. Very soon they leave me with some kind of rationalization in their own minds: "I didn't see that. I am not going to touch that with a barge pole. Let someone else do it."

I say to my doctor, "I can't go to any appointment with a specialist or schedule an operation when I'm in a 'down part' of my day. I can't stand up." She says, "Well maybe it would be good for them to see you 'this way'."

What does she not understand? I can't stand up. No matter how graphic I get, no one listens.

April 24th

Dear Carol,

I woke up yesterday morning and could hear the falling trill of an eagle's call as I lay in bed. It was so different from the usual morning birdcalls that I had to pay attention. This morning on my walk the smell of the damp humusy woods hit me so hard I had to stop. I wondered if I could walk blindfolded along that road that I have walked for the last seven years and tell where I was by smell. At certain times of the year it's easy.

Just now the Balm-of-Gilead are leafing out and their sticky poplar perfume, so sweet, wafts on the air. In earlier spring the daphne has that kind of fragrance.

Neighbours used to keep a billy goat in a dank hollow along their fence. He smelled, a musty odour both offensive and enticing. I often walked past him, oblivious to him until his odour hit me from behind. The billy goat is gone now. As I walk by his empty shed I sometimes get a phantom scent, like an amputee sensing a phantom limb. I miss the dark harmonics of his stink, a flirtation with animal essence.

It's been a long, cold, lonely spring. In the cool damp I seem to see more clearly than when the sun soothes me into a waking somnolence. The elderberry blow is forming on the elderberries. It is still green and tightly curled but soon it will be all white and lacy. I guess the word "blow" could be used for other flowers, but I have only seen it used for elderberries. I thought it was related to ideas of breath and inspiration (which seemed appropriate) but when I looked it up it turned out to be a variant on bloom. Oh well.

The new sword ferns emerge bent double, twisted like broken old men. They seem so dead it is hard to imagine them a twisted helix of life. The hop shoots have shot up like sinuous snakes against the chicken coop. They will leaf out soon but now they are all stretch and line. On the small red Japanese maple the new leaves are formed but still shrunken and distorted like ancient arthritic hands or the awkward groping fingers of newborns. This transitional time is so fired with energy and eagerness for life. The new leaves on the hazelnuts are crimped like Japanese silk. On the *magnolia sieboldii*, the leaves are tight like the beautiful hand-rolled cigarettes they call "bidis" in Nepal. These tensely coiled forms make the mature leaves seem almost flaccid and spent in comparison.

These days the world is as green as the Emerald City of Oz. Now suddenly there are pinpricks of shocking red: the greeny purple buds of the black currant have turned flaming scarlet. This whole season is green and red – the colours of new life. When I pull the maple seedlings that are everywhere in the perennial bed I see that below the ground their green stems turn to deep red, then pure white. The tree peonies are like an exercise in complementary colours or a thermodynamic satellite photo. The central veins on the leaves are the greenish tributaries draining reddish uplands, but the greens and reds are greyed and muted. The new leaves on the Anthony Waterer spirea come in a rosy red, then fade into pink-tinged green. The rhubarb is off and running, sturdy red stems holding up great green Limpopo leaves. Soon will come my favourite, the kiwi vine with the hairy red stems and the perfectly formed thick green leaves. The reds are never just red – they are orange-red, purple-red, pink-red, salmon-red, just as the greens are blue-green, yellow-green, grey-green.

The deer have got most of the tulips but there is one crimson one at the base of a great Douglas fir surrounded by Easter lilies that I don't remember planting. I love this flamboyance in tiny doses. Speaking of tulips, I am in love with their alchemical approach to colour. I've been watching some purple-black ones come into their fullness. First the purple shows up as a faint edge outlining the green outer petals. Gradually that green is suffused with purple and then finally it is truly saturated with tone. It is so subtle I'm glad there are several in a clump in different stages so I can see the progression and prove to myself that I'm not hallucinating. Maybe this is an image for each of us moving into the confidence to become our true selves – letting our true colours show. The camas are doing it too. What a gift.

This past weekend was finally warm and I managed to plant the peas, fava beans, spinach and kohlrabi. It was so warm, in fact, that I could imagine the spinach bolting as soon as it leafed out. Today, though, is damp and miserable again, so I probably don't have to worry. Meanwhile the tomatoes and squash I started on the window sill are outgrowing their peat pots. If the season continues this slow, I can imagine a geriatric ward for sprawling seedlings.

I've been taking photos of the fruit trees as they blossom, and wondering if I will be able to remember which is which when the slides come back. Each is quite distinctive, though they all follow the same theme of five petals (I think) with subtly delicate to outrageously decadent stamens in their centres. Each blossom lies in its own way on the branch, hangs from stems (in the case of cherries) or sits in pert clumps (in the case of pears). Each tree is like a mini-drama unfolding. It leaves me no time for the TV soaps.

Yesterday the rain came down in torrents. The wind gusted madly, first sending flurries of cherry blossoms, then blizzards of cherry blossoms that speckled the grass and the rhubarb leaves, sticking to the outdoor chairs and the old worn table. This morning the sun gleamed behind the branches of the wild cherry, at its peak of bloom, illuminating it as it lay against the sky like fine sheets of transparent vellum. The sun is still out but it's raining again and getting greyer by the minute. Rudy just let the mules out. They are jumping around kicking up their heels with uncharacteristic abandon. The peas I planted a few days ago have all popped up to the surface, buoyed by the rain, but Rudy reports he's poked them back down. What a crazy season.

Take care. Love, Dorothy

April 25th *Cold and rainy again*

Dear Dorothy,

When Ron and I come home, as we turn into the drive we both audibly sigh and say aloud, "Get ready." At the curve the car goes under the canopy of trees and, as if we entered an old "Twilight Zone" episode, we are alone in a primeval forest. It is the same glorious feeling as when one dives into water – the very reality of our existence instantly changed into a world of altered visual sensation, freedom of motion and silence.

I remember so clearly the early days when I was guiding the building of the house and struggling to save the plant life. For the old Carol this task would have been great fun. But this disease I live with leaves me no toughness, no energy, so it was a Herculean task. Except for my friend and builder, and one like-minded tree faller, every other person involved seemed determined to remove the growth. I still hear their voices: "I can't manoeuvre my machine with those scrubby bushes there"; "I can't pull those fallen trees with that awful thicket there"; "I can't get the cement truck close enough with those wretched trees there. Those are *weed* trees and should be removed." I had never heard so many denigrating terms used to describe flora, or met so many big-mouthed "experts" who thought that they would run roughshod over me with their threats of doom and gloom.

At 8 a.m. on my fiftieth birthday I remember meeting with an independent hydro contractor whom I hired to put in the 400-foot electrical line. In those early morning hours we trudged back and forth through the rough, tree-filled terrain, him saying, "All this *has* to go." He motioned with big sweeps, his attitude pure frustration. Back and forth we went, me being firm but quickly getting fatigued, my energy draining by the second. He became more physically agitated, but verbally polite. Finally he told me that the project would be scrutinized by B.C. Hydro's guidelines and the dreaded on-the-spot inspection. His eyes rolled sideways as he shrugged with his wait-and-see attitude. I had the swath cut by a very sensitive tree faller who did exactly what I wanted. I told him that Ulysses (the giant arbutus) was designated a heritage tree by the local historical society. Whatever it took. I passed the inspection easily.

I treasured this land. I loved every plant and tree. I would push through the thickness of the growth, finally emerging into the brightness of the open Queen Anne's lace field. I wanted the land exactly as it was. At my request, the builder cleared a spot in the growth only six feet wider than the house dimensions. He cut every board exactly to dimension and numbered them, in his workshop miles away, so that there was no mess and tramping of the land. When we later wrapped a six-foot deck around the house, it actually touched the wild crabapple trees I had fought to preserve. The old pear tree determined the curve of the deck by its presence. The wild rose I saved is now one of the wonders of this place, almost as tall as the house. It provides perching and hiding places for the hundreds of birds that line up to feed on the back deck.

Most often, developers trying their best to wring every penny of profit from the land do the butchering of the growth and the raping of the soil. Scrape off everything, build that house, and up goes the FOR SALE sign. The luckless buyer spends the rest of his life making it look like it did before Mr. Bulldozer had his way. In one hour a bulldozer can remove what will take you twenty or thirty years to replace, the soil structure lost forever.

My builder was most patient with my wishes. He was often inconvenienced by the growth, and his truck suffered indignities circumventing trees and trying to manoeuvre without a gravel drive. I eventually had to put a gravel driveway in. It took six years to cover the scars of that. Now it appears as it was in the beginning, a grassy track through the woods.

I remember the advice of one visitor, a long-time forest harvester, who said, "Don't be anxious to clean the place up. Let the trees fall and stay. The undergrowth will cover it, and all that you leave feeds the forest floor." As Ron and I studied the birds and became acquainted with their ways, their needs and habits, we value the bush. We now use all yard clean-up and pruning wastes to make forest piles that eventually compost. In the meantime they make nesting sites for the quail. We weave the branches of trees and bushes that we remove into the Leylandi hedges as well as the wire fences, blending fence and hedge.

I have been thinking of our valley that I've watched for so many years: of the wild areas where the mallards come each year; of the fields where the deer always lie, sometimes the grass so high only their ears show. I have been watching the demise of a lovely old barn that is slowly descending, returning itself to the soil. Fruit trees hide its weathered and rotting boards. Each time we drive past the spot, I am thankful no bulldozer has been there.

The most interesting part of watching this area is seeing the properties change hands and how differently people treat their land. It is always wonderful when I see a property change from a sow's ear to a silk purse. One five-acre parcel on Telegraph Road comes to mind. The first owners cleared a cube out of the trees and built a house so close to the road that dust flew into the front room. Each of the outbuildings faced the road, squared to all the others. There was no attention to the lay of the land or existing plant growth, no beauty – nothing to feed the soul.

But things change, and surprising things happen. The next owners were braver than I would have been. In the course of a year they moved the house back and angled it facing due south, on a slope that helps catch the sun's rays. They added an adjacent greenhouse and a charming roofed porch. This property is now a jewel in the woods with fenced orchards and little gardens and trees to help shield the house from the road.

This is definitely the time of the most delicate and fresh fragrances of the year. My all-time favourite is the leafing of the wild roses, a scent so heady and strange. Sometimes as I walk along the roadside I am stopped in mid-thought: I look up and see there is a rose bush.

I saw a frog leap into the pond, so we keep our fingers crossed.

Love, Carol

May 6th

Dear Carol,

The grass is as high as a goose's thigh, or a gosling's midriff, for that matter. The chicks virtually swim in it. I've pulled off the blackened magnolias so the branches are graced by pale porcelain blooms and the frost-frozen corpse buds seem part of another life.

After the great wind I noticed the road edge strewn with coral sheaths, like cuticles. fallen from the bigleaf maples. I began to observe more carefully how the leaf buds form as great phallic pouches sheathed like swords in red codpieces. What a show! Each sheath is an overlapping of scales, like an armadillo's shell. The sheaths elongate, then the red scales separate to reveal the clenched green leaves within. Eventually the red pouches become vestigial organs, pennants to the miracle of the new growth. After the wind it was these pennants I found along the road. I looked then at the newly forming leaves on a small Japanese maple, which will have fine tendril leaves, and there they were again, a long, thin version of the red pennants.

So I am struck by this world, which does its thing whether I stop to look or not. I am struck by the thrill of seeing something that has always been there but that I have been blind to. And then I feel an irrational panic that these road edges will reveal themselves so thoroughly that there will be no great discoveries left. But in fact the world is an ever-unfolding mystery.

I think of these unfolding details as the gateway to infinity and wonder. Two springs ago I made an artist's book inspired by a series of quotes about this idea. William Blake said, "Singular and particular detail is the foundation of the sublime." Rav Kook wrote, "Every part of the vegetable world is singing a song." The details these days are sharp and fast, not slow and muffled in fog as they were in the long winter months. I am exhausted and exalted.

I just came across a myth from the Kabbalah again, about the light of the world being stored in a great clay vessel. It cracks and the shards impregnated with light are scattered around the world until that time when we can reassemble them into wholeness. If I were to describe spring it would be as a time when the sparks are flying and I am running after them, trying to see, trying to catch them, hold them. Images of fireflies in a dusky meadow or sparklers held aloft by light-drunk kids, or me.

It seems exaggerated this spring, maybe because the days are still so cool and there has been so much rain. There's no incentive to be out doing, but the looking has been spectacular.

I was moved by your description of how you fought to save the woods around your house and I was impressed by your fortitude in standing up to all those men. We had almost the opposite story. We had admired this farm for several years before I answered a tiny ad in the Victoria paper and realized it was this place. The old house was charming, set back down a long driveway with big open fields and a large locust tree in front. By great luck we bought it and then began to soften it up. When we were first here there was nothing between the house and the chicken coops but two lilacs, one pear tree, one apple and one plum. We have planted and planted, we've let the hawthorns along the driveway grow, we've put in the orchards and the berries and wild roses along the driveway. In those early days the grass quickly burnt to brown in the summer heat. Now all the new trees keep the water table higher and things stay green all summer. It is a long slow process, but the other day I noticed that the dogwood I transplanted when I was pregnant twenty years ago is now almost as tall as the maple, and the wild cherry tree which was a sucker dug up from a friend's backyard is enormous.

We moved in here on July 1 almost twenty-three years ago. The following spring Rudy told me sadly that the huge locust in front of the house, the weeping willow and another tree were all dead. Fortunately he was wrong; they weren't dead, he was just impatient. Since then many things have died, trees and shrubs, chicks and lambs. Storms have cracked off great chunks of trees, horses have rubbed young persimmons into oblivion, careless watering in the long hot time has choked off trees planted in out-of-the-way corners. But mostly there is increasing life and richness and detail. Most plants hold tight to life, given a little understanding and even half a chance.

Despite this expressed optimism, I am in despair over the loss of wildflowers in our woods. For years I kept finding more and more calypso orchids. There was one path where the trilliums were thick as clotted cream. These last few years there have been fewer, but I thought that maybe the season was bad. This year their numbers are so reduced I feel I am in mourning whenever I go into the woods. I don't know what's causing this. I blame it on the mules that graze back there during midsummer, but I don't really know if that's the reason. And I feel grief that the woods that I have so loved have suffered under our tenancy.

I find great pleasure in this paper conversation we've been sharing. It

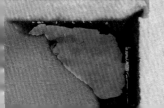

has become a particular outlet for a kind of thought I rarely share. There aren't many places in the world with time and space for this type of meandering thought. It has created light and shadow in the grey winter doldrums. It has heightened the moments of revelation.

One of my great pleasures this spring has been watching the colours shift – the magnolias start out deep pink and gentle off into a pearly white; the tulips start grey-green and suffuse through into the deep orange, purple-black or true red that they were meant to be; the dogwood flowers begin greeny yellow and move into rich ivory, and so many leaves start out rusty red and gradually turn towards green. I remember those old time-lapse films that showed flowers opening, and would like to make footage of these colour transformations.

I don't know why the vegetable world sings to me – I am not a dedicated hauler of manure or garden maintainer. I am mostly interested in following the transformational thread: the unfurlings, the suffusings, the dying offs, the great drama of buds and leaves and seed heads. Lately I notice the geese standing on one leg, then creakily stretching the other one, unfurling the curled up webbed foot like the maples unfurl their new leaves. Finally they place the full foot flat on the ground, stretch their necks and squawk, extending their wedged tongues between their yellow bills. Not much else to report. Rudy is on the rampage, cutting off branches infested with the dreaded tent caterpillars to burn in the stove while I am planning a class about spinning paper, thinking about the metaphor of webs and the magic of animal architecture. Amazing that two people can see the same world from two such different vantage points.

Take care, Dorothy

When I got up from typing yesterday and got undressed to shower before my swim, I had jolts of numbness down my left leg, which has been my good leg during all this. Each time I bent over, a jot would travel from my spinal area to my left big toe, numbing the leg. Well, I had a spontaneous panic attack, heart beating so hard, feeling hot and weakened. Within an hour, having talked this through with Ron, I was reconciled, sort of, to whatever comes next. I cannot control this new development, whatever it means. I can only continue to be as active as I can, get through each day and find what is good in it.

Yesterday's appointment with the podiatrist went well. He was very knowledgeable and he looked me straight in the eyes, like looking into me. (It is so seldom that I feel a health practitioner is really "with me," not writing notes or answering phone calls or giving me the feeling of wanting to get on with the next appointment.) He listened to my story (much abbreviated), looked at my collection of orthotic shoes and checked the pulses on both feet. In my right foot, the worse foot, the pulse is barely acceptable, where it used to be excellent in both feet. As I talked about my toes and feet, my back and the fatigue, I said several times, "You must hear this all the time, since all you work with is feet." He said no. He said, "Your feet are not giving you the problems. Your body is giving your feet the problems. You obviously have systemic problems. The feet are merely signals that something is very wrong and you need to get yourself to a very, very good internist and have many tests."

He thinks my symptoms are from something like Lupus, connective tissue disease, Reynard's disease, something in the blood, because the blood platelets are clumping. God, I do not want to hear this. I have had mysterious symptoms for *so long that it is a relief to hear someone be so straightforward, but it is also frightening. Other doctors have said, "You have something grave going on here," but when the tests have shown nothing alarming, they say, "You are carrying on wonderfully despite everything." I have never been checked out thoroughly and exhaustively. Since my GP told me this podiatrist is "the best," she will have to follow up with more thorough testing. I went immediately to a nearby lab and had blood drawn. There is something going on that is far beyond Chronic Fatigue Syndrome or a ruptured disc.*

May 12th *Where is spring?*

Dear Dorothy,

I reread Robert Frost's poem "Mending Wall." I wonder what he would be inspired to write if he lived here in our area of neither farm nor suburb. I listened to an audio book tape of *Wingfield Farm* and laughed myself silly because it was so hilarious and reminds me of the situations and characters I have encountered over the years in the Cowichan Valley. Sorry, R.F., but here in this valley I have to agree with your neighbour who said "Good fences make good neighbours," though I might rephrase that to "Good fences make better neighbours."

I thought of this poem the other night when we were brought bolt upright by one of our neighbours using noisy equipment. When these things happen we rush out to peer through our fences to see what they are up to. We live in what may seem to be paradise, but in fact we live here with an underlying unease, never knowing when our little sanctuary will be put at risk. Right now we are waiting to see what our neighbours to the south, who own three plus acres, are going to do. When you live in a city on a lot, you pretty much know what you have.

Likewise when you live on a farm, surrounded by your 160 acres. This area, however, is in constant flux, with properties frequently changing hands (we have four properties which are adjacent to some part of our two acres) and potential changes to neighbouring zoning, which is a great fear. We often feel like we are in a castle, constantly watching our walls for invaders, heating the tar and digging the moat deeper and day-dreaming of stocking an alligator or two. It is a quiet watchfulness.

I learned about living in the country, farmette style, when I moved to Briarwood subdivision, a cluster of two-acre parcels with forty homes on what was formerly a farm. The first time a dog bit Holden as he was coming home from school, I learned about how dog owners react to their dogs' "bad deeds." They hide. Another neighbour's German shepherd maimed our mother duck while she sat on her eggs. We nursed her, doubting that she would live, but she raised thirteen ducklings and limped for the rest of her life. The German shepherd's owners said, "He never goes off our property," though he was caught with bloody duck feathers in his mouth on our property. Then they said, "Well, *you* have to get a dog so other dogs won't come onto your property."

In eleven years we saw neighbours come and go and we were constantly running an unofficial dog training school. Young, unsupervised dogs not tied up on their properties would frolic in our fenced land, chasing the chickens and ducks and running my sweet, fat pet sheep. I can see Hank yet, going out, grabbing the dog by the scruff, whipping his ass and throwing him over our fence yelling, "*Bad dog, go home!*"

We would sit out on lawn chairs on a late summer evening, with pop-corn, watching our neighbours "walking the dogs" around Briarwood circle. Neighbours with two huge dogs each on a leash would start out walking the dogs in one direction. On the other side of the circle another person with their dog or dogs, most often off leashes, would set out. Somewhere they all would meet and the inevitable "dog wars" happened. The sounds were ferocious, and the owners, unable to control the maddened beasts, yelled epithets about their counterparts' parentage.

I've been jumped on and knocked down by a 200-pound dog and been hit in the crotch so many times by sniffing pointy-nosed dogs that I've learned automatic defence postures. "No, no Cujo! Don't do that!" the dog owners croon. "He just loves people and is as gentle as a lamb," they reassure me. "Here, here sweetie-kins, come here, come here!!!" is the last thing I hear as we pass each other.

One year one of the centre properties of the circle changed hands and I saw massive, no-nonsense, professionally built fences go up swiftly. I said to Hank, "Now there are thoughtful, smart dog owners." Inside the fence two vicious-sounding German shepherds and another large dog raced from fence end to fence end of the two acres, unable to bite ass. Months later, while visiting my neighbour Mary, I said that her next-door neighbours showed wonderful responsibility in building the fences to contain their dogs. Then Mary told me that the very day after they moved in, she had invited them for tea. She is soft-spoken, neat as a pin, with white hair. During afternoon tea, with little cakes and polite conversation, she had said to them, "Oh, I see that you have dogs. If you find that they are dead of poisoning, do not look around for the person who did it. It will have been me. I will poison them the first time I find them on my property." You would have to have known Mary to understand that she could carry this off. The day after the tea party, the fence went up. I admired Mary so much, and her words of advice and collected wisdom still ring in my head.

At Briarwood, during those eleven years, my only other complaint with neighbours was a continuing battle over the road. Against all common sense and reason, our neighbours treated little Briarwood lane as a four-lane highway, scooping off all growth on the generous road allowances and digging ditches for a one-hundred-year flood that was never to come on that high, porous plateau. I think of those halcyon days as preparation for the much harder struggles I would have here, both personally and in defence of this land. But that is another story.

⤨

My elder son phoned me on Mother's Day for a talk, and I found out that he was doing landscaping on his small acreage in Nanaimo. As we talked I could hear my influence in what he was doing with the land, and was gratified. He was planting indigenous plants on his hard-to-grow-on soil, porous stuff on porous rock, with short water supply. I wrote him a letter, with drawings, on how to transplant more successfully in dry areas, where constant watering in the summer is not an option. I also gave him some ideas of what to plant.

What I notice this year of no spring is that the natural flora is doing wonderfully. I see new plants: vanilla leaves (sweet after death) where they weren't, along with a nest of wild lily-of-the-valley, as well as water plantain, enhancing the shallower part of the pond.

Love, Carol

May 29th

Dear Carol,

Congratulations on being a new grandmother. Such a powerful passage for all of you. It feels like the perfect timing. Since I left for North Carolina and returned, the whole earth has shifted. Before I left I was documenting the birth pangs, the tiny crumpled leaves wizened like translucent newborns as they burst the bonds of their constricting buds and slowly stretched into fullness. The earth is now at ten centimetres, fully open and flying leaf flags from every balustrade and tower. This lush greenness is almost anti-climactic. I miss the drama of becoming in this complacent comfort of arrival. Here, as in my art, I am more interested in process than product. But the sun has been out most of the past three days and it is shining now. And for me the feeling of sun on skin is the true reward after the long mouldering months.

While I was in North Carolina I got to play with my favourite toy, the Xerox machine. I pulled up a clump of clover by the roots, placed it on the Xerox glass and ran some clear acetate through. The clover emerged – depth, nuance and root hairs – as if from the hand of a great draftsman. I used a Xerox image of a pulled-up clump of grass as the basis for a tiny book I made with a text I quoted you last letter: "Every part of the vegetable world is singing a song." It was all a bit mad since I had treated the cover paper with something very oily like floor wax or varnish so the glue wasn't anxious to stick. These little books (I made twenty of them for an edition) are already self-destructing. The label glued onto the cover fell into a friend's wine as he was looking at it last night. It is the life cycle all over again.

I am not of a very archival bent. I won't be unhappy if this little book passes through a few hands and then falls away like autumn leaves. While I was teaching I talked about the Inuit idea of art's relation to life. The Inuit word for poetry has the same root as the word "to breathe." Yet the Inuit speak of their carvings as a kind of excrement, a by-product of life process. I love this paradox – that art is everything and nothing at the same time.

Yesterday I planted the dry beans. I'm a little nervous that the seeds may all rot and then it's a chore to replace them, but I was more nervous that if I didn't get them planted, they would not have time to ripen. Mostly I planted old varieties that I know – midnight black turtle, agate pinto, ruckle – but I was transfixed by a new one, mojave, that is a patched pattern of magenta and cream. They look so passionate – will they taste of passion? I am also anticipating harvesting them to see the inside of the pods. The dried pods are like silken whispers mirroring the colour of the jewels within. Have you ever read *The Tale of Genji*? It is full of such crazy subtleties and observations of colour and the natural (and unnatural) world.

I spent long hours this past weekend weeding the rows I planted before I went away. I try to remember when there was a clear enough day to have planted them and can only recall rain and grey, but there must have been one day because the peas, broad beans, onions and spinach are all there in their rows. Weeding the peas was a disappointment since it showed up how poor the germination was on two varieties. Oh well. The beets and spinach, radicchio and turnip greens are thick. Also the lettuces. I planted the corn in a new spot where the nasturtiums were rampant last summer. I plan to take a firmer hand and not let them go quite so mad, but I also thought if the corn got a good start it might be a good support for raging nasturtium tendrils.

The lilacs have come and almost gone while I've been away. Lilacs are such an emblem of old farm life. All across this continent old purple lilacs mark homesteads that have since fallen away. There were three here when we bought the farm – the old kind, nothing flashy. One in particular has been blighted for years – flowers and leaves form and then shrivel into blackness. Every year I think I will do something to remedy the situation but the season passes, I prune out the spent flowers and forget. This year, writing to you, I make myself a promise not to forget. I've planted a new lilac, which is still small. The blooms are so monstrous and double they bend the frail branches almost to the ground. I think I prefer the simple blooms of the old-fashioned variety.

I must have written to you about medlars last fall. Now I've been watching them bud up. The buds are long and slender with attenuated finger-forms that twist together at the ends. As they open, these fingers are like horns surrounding the white blossom. The medlar fruits, even when they are round and plump brown, have little horny protuberances at the blossom end. This mysterious continuity of form intrigues me – like infants who are already themselves in the first hours of their birth. Some are jumpy and tightly wound, others are placid and serene, and these basic personality traits seem to remain with them through their lives.

Since writing these letters to you, I've begun to understand Jane Austen's heroines endlessly writing letters. I used to wonder what they had to say. Now I know. The pleasure of this kind of correspondence

about the tiny dramas of the garden is almost a lost art, choked off by the telephone, given the final blow by fax and e-mail. In the world of artists' books there is an ongoing debate and panic about libraries becoming wholly electronic. Meanwhile interest in beautiful editions on gorgeous paper increases. Maybe this ever-faster communication will allow snail mail to carve out its own niche for a slower kind of communication, which is about love of the moment and process and words.

I was just in the pea patch – most of the new pea plants are twined onto the mesh netting but a few lay sprawled in the dirt. They reminded me of us humans. There they lay grasping at straws (one had twined its tendrils around tiny bits of straw mulch, the blind leading the blind). They clung to each other, their peripatetic shoots frenetically snarled into useless knots. As I headed them back to the netting, their delicate tendril fingers seemed to have a consciousness that sensed a truer support. Delicately, almost imperceptibly they curved to the fine mesh. It reminded me of the way infants with eyes closed respond to human touch. Interesting how this letter keeps coming around to babies.

Congratulations again. We're thinking of you and that wild new grandson.

Love, Dorothy

June 4th   *Windy, 56 degrees*

Dear Dorothy,

I have been chuckling ever since we exchanged seedlings: you giving me tiny artichokes and tomatoes while I handed you the videotape of my new grandson. I've come upon something totally unexpected: the grandmother phenomenon. Just when I thought I had life figured out, this new thing happens. I carry pictures of him with me and track down acquaintances in the Thrifty's parking lot. I'm shamefaced, remembering friends sending me pictures of their children and grandchildren and me wanting to see *them*, my friends, not those pod-person strangers. I remember a friend falling in love at the ripe age of fifty-four and then understanding what had happened to so many people he knew over his lifetime. He had thought them quite mad — what is this "falling in love"? With a red face, he was most thrilled with this new and wonderful life gift. Without even a hint of a blush, I carry my grandson's pictures.

On the day after Caspian's birth I wandered around the yard, planning the perfect spot where he could be married. Imagine? If he married at an early twenty-five I would be eighty-two and if he is a wiser thirty-five I would have to hang around until ninety-two. These figures now make new life markers. The death of our last parent is certainly a time we all know is coming and usually have some warning about. However, planning a wedding of a grandchild? I start dreaming and it is all about the land, the outdoors, nature, the saneness and perfection of this acreage. Maybe he will be like me and love all this. Maybe he will be the one to make a market garden in the front field.

His birth makes everything seem sweeter and more precious — how can this be? I walk under the arbours, seeing him playing in the sandbox (not yet there), seeing him rolling down the gentle slopes of grass, seeing him standing there full grown. The birth of this boy has me reaching out to touch the hands of my grandparents to introduce them. But most of all I want to put this child into my mother's and father's arms. An emptiness surfaces and leaves me in tears. I have no one to share this with. No one to stare into his eyes and seek familial similarities. No one to say, "He is just like your great uncle," or "He reminds me of my brother at that age." I search my family photos for a likeness of him. The faded and cloudy reels of my life show distorted images from the past.

The day of his birth, May 23, marked the change in our weather: from winter to summer. I rushed around so fast to pick things that are blooming that I hardly had time to look. The day of his birth the chickadees came out of their nest box (the ones we saw being harassed by the raccoon), coaxed by their loud-mouth parents: "Come out, come out, this is the end of your babyhood." Baby birds are all over: rufous-sided towhees, looking nothing like their parents except for a white mark on their sassy tails (the tail movement gives them away), sparrows, starlings, finches, chickadees, robins, crows, red-winged blackbirds, cowbirds, wrens and so many in flight I can't identify them. Groups of two to four birds chase their parents, begging for food. I thought of how each time one of our grown children visit, I say, as they are leaving, "You always have a place to stay (indicating the guest trailer) and food to eat when you come."

Funny we use the phrase "Empty Nest" to indicate an emptiness humans may feel when their children leave home. Birds coax their young out of the nest without mercy, and then are chased to feed the fledglings (or so it seems from our perspective). The whole process takes very little time, and no emotion. The insistent peeps from the fluffy bird babies are very compelling – like the human baby's cry – parents must respond. We still have a robin nesting above the bedroom door, on the power-line entrance into the house, so have to tread gently there. We can never go out the back door because the feeders are in constant use. This morning I *had* to use the back door, so knocked ever so gently to warn the birds I was coming. (Get that? Knocking before entering the birds' domain.) We are so closely nestled by the trees and bush, we go slightly mad listening to the baby birds squeak and peep, on and on, day after day. I am tempted to wear my industrial ear protectors, but hate to miss this short-run drama.

On the day Caspian was making his entrance to the outside world, Ron was building the arbour for the giant honeysuckle next to the front door. This arch, made of one cedar post and two treated crosspieces, has changed the whole feeling of the front door and the deck. I open the front door and sit under this small roof, smelling the honeysuckle and watching the bird nursery antics in the orchard. This morning I saw a cluster of pin-head-sized spiders newly hatched, spinning their guy wires over the potted trifid, as if decorating it. The sun hit their golden bodies and their fine webs. We named the honeysuckle arbour Caspian's Arch. Immediately it has become a gathering place: we took photos of Ron's sons under it, after a celebration of Ben's birthday and Hugh's high-school graduation. This will definitely be the year of the arbours. Ron has built three and is now tackling the Bird Bush. It long ago swamped the east end of the house, huge steps and all. He plans a giant arch, made with rebar struts and wood, which will make a long tunnel through the bush.

I love this year, now that summer is here, although I feel as though I have been in a coma for months. Maybe everyone else had spring while I slept? Something is definitely wrong. It feels odd and leaves me off bal-ance. We are using plant volunteers to fill whatever spaces need flowers. This is not a good year for volunteers. The nasturtiums are there but look like wizened old men. Beatrice's strawflower volunteers came up but the quail were so greedy for new greens that they ate them. The quail also ate your asters as they came up. When we realized what was happening, Ron covered the beleaguered new growth, but now the clumps are all uneven and missing here and there. Whether the weather or the quail, who knows? So far there are no accidental squash, but it has not been warm enough. For the first year ever, I find myself nervously looking for them — if even just one appears, all will be right in my world. The rose apple, which came out so slowly, is still blooming. It bloomed in only two places and the flowers have opened at least a month apart! I've marked the blooms with tags to watch the apples form, should I be so lucky.

Ron's daily job is cutting out the tent caterpillar nests. As if this cold and wet spring wasn't enough, this seems to be a great year for the tent caterpillars. I hate them: in the sun, they insanely flick their bodies back and forth, clustering on those repulsive web nests. They drop from the trees onto me, and I feel them crawling around in my hair or on my clothes or even on the bed covers. Gad! When Holden was three and four and five he used to play with tent caterpillars; he would come in the house with a handful of his friends, all squirming in a furry knot. It made me nauseous. He treated me like a traitor when he caught me killing them. At his age it was impossible to explain why reverence for all life may have some exceptions. I now wonder about this more and more.

This past year of death and birth I see our world so confused, the world population so out of control. Not an easy problem to deal with. In my younger years, when I thought that things were simple to fix, I felt that China, at least, was making a wise attempt at controlling their population. Little did I know that it would be such a disaster. I watched "The Passionate Eye" on television the night before last, watching until I could take no more: horrific images of Chinese orphanages filled with girl babies, thrown away by parents seeking boy children since they are allowed only one child. I am filled with rage, revulsion, disbelief and hopelessness. We grapple with the questions of birth control, women's rights and the right to die. Ron assures me that this craziness and imbalance on our planet is only a temporary state: that things will right themselves.

❦

Our yard plans have shifted and changed with the tumultuous spring. We are guided by lack of funds, my back problems on top of the disease, and the reluctant spring. We are having fun with what is already here. Our plans include more arches, made of the trees themselves. We will train the witch trees (wild crabapples) into tunnels. On mornings like these I can feel very guilty, me here in paradise with all the turmoil and suffering and war and devastation elsewhere. Even more reason to look and see the wonder of it all. Here, in our space under the canopy of trees, we lead a sweet life.

I walk out into the midst of this land and smell the heavenly fragrances. I realize the world is right here. The earth has billions of stories and this is just one of them.

Love, Carol

P.S. The pond has healed, is full of life and lily pads, mottled purple water irises and wild yellow swamp irises are blooming. There are beautiful husks shed by dragonfly larvae on the stems of cattails. The surviving fish are becoming giants and one frog holds court on the leaves of a no-name water plant. I saw a fat snail floating upside down, as they do, his underbelly like translucent amber. Cattails have taken hold and spread themselves in such a pattern – no artist could do better. I see Evie, the queen of the lilies, has begun to put out red flower buds underneath the water. If only the pond and all nature could hold at this point, just for a while.

CAROL'S JOURNAL

From Monday's visit to the urologist I learned that the urinary problems I have been having for almost a decade all fall into a category called Interstitial Cystitis, which is common among women with Chronic Fatigue Syndrome. For ten years I have been describing what is happening and it always has been dismissed or misdiagnosed because it's so easy to prescribe antibiotics. I find most doctors don't have the time to really listen, and even if they do, they don't remember from one time to another to string facts together. But when I told it all again to this new doctor, she identified it as Interstitial Cystitis. I had the information about this already and had finally figured it out, sort of. Now it's official.

Next week I have an appointment with a neurologist / internist at a hospital in Victoria and already I'm wearing myself out with worry. I know I'll have to lie down afterwards. If I just pretend to faint, I'll bet they will find a cot in a corner somewhere. I am sick and tired of health facilities never being set up for almost-bedridden people like me. The staff act horrified that I have to lie down.

Can you believe this? People with as much fatigue and down time as I have are usually staying in health facilities, or else they are sent by ambulance. There is no in-between care for people like me.

⌒

All that I am doing, however commendable, is not making me better. I do not know what is going on, and don't seem to get any answers. So yesterday Ron and I decided to do the pool routine every day, turning this place into a health spa. Ron will do more and more manipulation and massage and I will concentrate on therapeutic movements and do less of everything else. I have already given up most writing. I cannot use any of my limited energy except to try to get muscle tone back. I am losing range of motion and live in constant discomfort from muscle strain and pain and numbness. No one can tell me what to do because they don't know what is going on. We use the advice we get and we try our very best.

June 10th

Dear Carol,

A few days ago I was walking back down the driveway with the mail. There is a place where the hawthorn trees grow from each side, almost forming an arch. Usually I am distracted, trying to figure out who's writing to me, but for some reason that day I felt the tree's architecture as a doorway into this spot of earth we've been messing with these last twenty-three years, this secret garden. Then I walked through the "arch" and looked up at the giant locust tree in front of the house. It has always been the anchor for the house, shaped in an elm-like vase form. It is a brittle tree, which drops hunks of bark and chunks of branches in wind-storms. Last summer Rudy became alarmed at the terrible split that was cracking down between the two major branches. We had a tree man come and do surgery. Now there is a great blunt stub on one side where the lost member used to stretch in a gentle arc.

Standing there I felt the loss, felt the phantom limb as if I were the locust. I felt the tree as a metaphor for us struggling humans, somewhat maimed by what was doled out to us, but compensating, still leafing out every spring, creating summer shade, giving the birds a resting spot and vantage point, providing support for a thorny blackcap vine. Mossy and warty, the locust stands as it must have stood these last seventy or eighty years. A while ago we printed an old negative we found when we were tearing up old linoleum in Cicely's room. It showed the house with its original siding, a small picket fence and the locust. There were two locusts then, one on either side of the path to the front door, both just saplings. There was another by the back door when we bought the farm but it was diseased so we took it down. Now there is only this one. It would limp like a three-legged dog if it could walk, but as with people, I try to embrace its vitality, to see the tree's awkward stump as an emblem of its own particular story. I wish it many more years.

⌒

We too have been battling the tent caterpillars. It's so ironic. I have been working a lot lately with the metaphor of spiders and webs, with the idea of the artist producing her work from what she spins from her body. So here we are surrounded by these luxuriant webbed nests and I am revolted. Rudy is assiduous in attacking them on the fruit trees but he has given up on trees and shrubs that merely produce beauty. They are thick on the weedy hawthorn trees. The caterpillars cloak the ends of the branches in sticky gauze. Then they sit on their webs waving their front ends, a grisly come-on. Looked at close up they have their own kind of beauty – a fine diamond-back pattern in subtle onyx colours. They lie there on the webs, jammed tight together, writhing gently. I can't help but think of the garter snake pits we saw last summer in Manitoba. As their numbers increase we find more and more lounging singly or in pairs on leaves of the wild cherry, the black currants, the rosa rugosa, the flowering quince.

These caterpillars don't seem to do anything, not even eat. They just lie – leaden, inert. Are these the front-runners staking out new colonies, waiting for reinforcements to set up satellite stations in the outer reaches, or have they been on active duty in voracious eating frenzies and they've been granted well-earned R&R on a tropical beach? These wretched eating machines strip and devour the green balm we've been so hungry for. When they're through they leave behind an indigestible architecture – tough structural veins that stand bereft like the ruined carcass of a great cathedral. They climb the chicken wire that protects the rhubarb and the strawberries and hang there stranded like beached whales. As far as I can see they don't eat wire. Sometimes I pick them off and squish them. Sometimes I just let them hang. It hardly seems to matter – they are so omnipresent this year – except in how it affects me. I don't like the act of killing, even tent caterpillars.

Years ago we had a black slug plague. They lay on the garden paths thick as iron filings. They were everywhere, eating and eating. I kept jars in the garden to throw them into, I cut them in half with scissors, I grabbed them two at a time and hurled them over the garden fence into the neighbours' woods, sending them on wild aerial honeymoons. A few weeks ago we visited friends on Thetis Island. It is very foresty there, filtered light between the big trees, prime slug country. The slugs feast on all the plants our friends cultivate. They stash pointed sticks in every bed for fast and ruthless skewering. At first when they were lamenting their slug wars I loftily said something about slugs being sentient beings, too. After a tour of their garden I was ready to engage in a slug-killing spree of my own.

All through the Himalayas, Tibetan Buddhists put up prayer flags and spin prayer wheels. The movement of the printed paper or cloth puts prayer into the world for the benefit of all sentient beings, dogs, yaks, crows, humans, even slugs and tent caterpillars. This is the trick, it seems to me – to remain compassionate even under siege. I remember a few summers ago when several Tibetan monks spent two weeks creating a sand mandala at the Victoria Art Gallery. One day a fly settled on the mandala and skittered around, destroying a part of the intricate pattern before the monks could gently remove it. Then patiently they repaired the shattered design. Could I learn, I wonder, to be compassionate to these revolting garden plagues? Obviously I have a long way to go.

The driveway roses are all in bloom, single rosy red and white with vibrant yellow centres. I suddenly had an urge yesterday to nibble a pink petal. It was strong flavoured and slightly bitter. It transported me back to childhood, when I loved to eat roses. When I was six I was flower girl at an aunt and uncle's wedding. After the wedding I put my bouquet of pink rosebuds in the icebox, as we called it then, planning to savour it the next day. Unfortunately, my older brother got there first and devoured it in the night. I was terribly disappointed. Anyway, I am so happy with the roses that I think I will take cuttings and try to get another six or eight plants to grow. It should be much faster than starting them from seed as I did with the ones there now.

I was very moved by your vision of Caspian's wedding in your garden. That is a very foreign idea for me, one that makes me envious. As urbanization increases all around us, I have desperate thoughts of moving I don't know where – somewhere farther from this ravening sprawling city beast (sounds like the tent caterpillars again). Meanwhile, since I am very bad at moving at all, we've planted walnut trees just in case we hang around for longer than I expect. We've been here long enough that we are now harvesting our walnut crop. Planting walnuts is always a commitment to the future since they take longer than almost anything else does to produce. When we planted them seventeen years ago, I was sure we'd be gone by now. We are planning to put in another pair of chestnuts (the mules and the deer ate the last pair) – another commitment to the future, and still we talk of moving. I wish I were better at either accepting things as they are and sending down my own more permanent roots or getting off my ass and trying out other pastures. I am a fence sitter, at least in this area. But I am looking forward to Caspian's wedding, since you seem better than I am at settling.

There is a monarch butterfly on the beauty bush just now, and the hummingbirds hang about the old weigela, sucking nectar. Both bushes, covered as they are these days with pink tubular flowers, must be like phlegmatic fleshy whores lying with thighs open for the fluttery winged ones. The bees too are everywhere, creeping over the roses and into the flowering shrubs. Yesterday in the post office there were several mailing envelopes filled with bees being shipped. The bees buzzed gently, swaddled in their postal wrappings, such a soothing summer sound.

I have done more investigation into the medlars. As the petals fall, I can see that the horns I described perch above what is now a slightly rising belly but which will swell into the ripened fruit. I told Rudy, who was not impressed since he'd figured this out long ago.

More than thirty years ago a college friend introduced me to Leonard Bernstein's musical version of Voltaire's *Candide*. It's playing in Vancouver this month and I just received tickets in the mail. I keep hearing the words of the final song that the protagonists sing after years of horrific misadventures and delusions: "And let us try before we die to make some sense of life. We'll build our house and chop our wood and make our garden grow." Strange and not strange how centuries ago in China poets expressed similar ideas about the garden's salutary powers. It is so easy to get disconnected from the sources of life in this crazy world (and probably in many previous crazy times over the last several millennia). The garden and the wild garden always bring me back to earth. It is also easy to fall into the trap of idealizing life in the garden. That's what the tent caterpillars are there for, I guess. What could be a more compelling image, after all, of the voracious energy of life? Food for thought.

Love, Dorothy

June 12th   5 *water lilies blooming*

Dear Dorothy,

The quote from your last letter, "And we will try before we die to make some sense of life…" started me thinking of so many things. Ron often says that here on this land he feels the happiest and most fulfilled of his life. Like he waited his whole life to really live. He loves building the house, moving the soil, planting the gardens. I feel that here at last I can live in my skin.

Yesterday, skillful larcenous landscapers that we are, we checked the remains of the old house site across from Mill Bay Centre. The house, a favourite of mine over the years, burned down a few seasons ago, leaving cement slabs, twisted pipes and a field of Sweet William. Among the ruins one lone, bright red poppy bloomed, one I have never seen. It now resides in my flower garden and continues to bloom despite its rude transplant. I walked around carefully surveying the site, surprised at what I found. A few large shrubs, an old apple tree and a path to the ravine and river, deep in the shadow of giant trees. There was a charming bridge, pushed over by children or fallen with age, rockwork walls and a seat, overgrown with ivy. Someone's former little area of peace, tranquillity and beauty, now a gathering spot of teenagers. I wished I could bend and pick up the litter.

We are experimenting with the trifids (the "dreaded Himalayan balsam") by pruning them back quite severely. They seed themselves thickly everywhere and then grow spindly and tall, eventually falling over in the rain or wind or during dry spells. I hope to find a way they can serve a purpose all summer long. Ron is such a gentle pruner. I said, "Prune lower or they will fall over." He said, "But they might die." I really laughed. Trifids die?

My outdoor bed is down at the pond, so this year I am discovering the development of cattails. Wow, when the wind blows those spring green sculptures at the top of the stems – the developing seed heads – clouds of green/yellow "smoke" erupt and float, only visible there for a few seconds. When I saw it the first time I thought of Ron, with his asthma, and wondered what would happen if he walked into that cloud of pollen. The heads are forming quickly, each day changing like art objects when the artist comes in nightly to work on his pieces. The forming heads resemble modernistic totem poles. It is rather late to start photographing and recording these breathtaking changes. That will be a project for next year.

This pond watching is amazing. Time passes very quickly, although action at the pond is very slow. I am learning the habits of the birds, some of whom spot me right off and fly on, others who never notice me and bathe themselves. The fish only catch my eye when their sudden change of direction and speed causes water displacement. My view is from bed level, of course. Dragonflies flit around with no apparent agenda. The frogs are the funny guys. One sits daily on the lily pads nearest me. He can sit for an hour without moving and then suddenly he jumps in and does the frog kick underwater, making the whole pond water quiver and undulate. This sets off the motion of the cattail stem reflections, which go crazy with various shapes. Meanwhile the birds stop on the Leylandi hedge at the north side of our property, coming in from the fields next door. I saw an eagle circling way high above the pond, making no wing movement at all, but he was around long enough for me to get a bit nervous. Yesterday on the landing field I saw a rabbit, the sun behind him, making his ears look fire-red and un-rabbitlike. The water irises have finished blooming, but the lilies are blooming every day, some here, some there, each lily flower lasting only a few days. There are so many greens around the pond I get lost in looking, my eyes focussing and refocussing on the countless forms. The colours are changed and made magical as they are reflected in the water.

It is almost the beginning of official summer and Ron hasn't planted out the seedlings. After all the talk about how much I could not do, I found ways, and have so many seedlings that I'm giving them away. Gardeners find a way. The nights are still often down to 42 or 43 degrees, seldom reaching 50. This is not a year for heat-loving plants.

Love, Carol

P.S. The accidental squash are out in more numbers this year than ever before. There are small seedlings, obviously melons from our salad makings. Ron has transplanted some of them, though none will have a chance to mature. Like you with paper-making and book-making, I know it is the process, not the product, which is important to me. Without our letter chats I never would have come to realize how important gardening and nature watching is to me. This is why I say, "Gardening is easy." I am interested only in the explorations, not so much the results. There are never really failures: only things to study and observe.

There are nine water lilies blooming and two frogs in the pond.

June 26th

Dear Carol,

I have been watching the purple grass along the fence. It is only purple when you are right there next to it. I must have passed it for years without seeing it. It starts out as a tight column, heathery in colour. As it matures it spreads like a Chinese brush, then arcs open into a feathery spray. If you move quickly past it you would assume it was green, which in a way it is, on a dusty green-purple continuum. It reminds me of the quality of emotions. We speak of anger but anger is often tinged with grief and grief may be tinged with remorse. Emotions too have a different colour depending on distance, right now versus one year ago, or ten years ago. The grass is most insistently purple in its earliest state, then fades to a lavender grey as it reaches middle age. I am watching to see what happens next.

Over the fence are several acres of grass just waiting to be cut by the mules and then baled so they have something to eat all winter. That cutting process is incredibly beautiful. Each path of the mower lays down a new swath; each pass changes the contours of the landscape. I have a sense of what it must have been like when the first plows broke the Prairie sod. But that is in the future. Now the grasses wave in the breeze, all green and grey-green and yellow-green and bone-bleached flax. Here and there are spots of purple vetch, drifts of daisies and patches of the dreaded yellow buttercups, which glint like gold in the sun. In places the grass is thick and thigh high. Looking down into it I have the sense of being above a great forest canopy. In other places it's sparse (Rudy would say it needs fertilizing and re-seeding) and I can see through the layers, as if looking into a woodland pond. I can see through the depths to the bottom and imagine a whole world of spiders and mice and snakes. When the hay is baled there is always at least one bale with a snake caught by surprise, trapped writhing and then finally still in the compacted grass. I can see through lateral layers as well. Moved by the wind, the grasses criss-cross in calligraphic transparencies. Each species of grass has its own particular rhythm. I can almost hear their voices, whispering, sighing or just silent. They speak to me, a polyglot of tongues.

I have been thinking about how the wild and the cultivated versions of the same plants bloom at the same time. Last year's radicchio, a type of chicory, has the same blue flowers on straggly gone-to-seed shoots as the rangy wild chicory along the road edges. The delicate sweet peas are up in the garden and the coarser wild ones along the driveway. But the wild versions fend for themselves, live in gravel, need no watering, return if the mood strikes (it usually does) or stay away. Their wildness feels like an atavistic call to make space for all that is wild inside me. Makes me think of the Claude Levi-Strauss book *The Raw and the Cooked*, which I think refers to this same dichotomy, and of the French word for raw vegetables: "crudités." So much of our most profound energy is in the raw, crude, uncultivated. "In wildness is the preservation of the earth" said that old Sierra Club poster. In the wild complexity, wild mysteries, in what we don't try to control but just allow, just love.

One of the things that intrigues me is knowing that each of my discoveries, the diamond patterns on the tent caterpillars, the purple on the grasses, is well known to experts in caterpillars and grasses. Each year I see things I have never noticed before and yet all of it is probably catalogued and categorized in scholarly tomes somewhere. This is freedom, to discover each in our own meandering time the details that stop us and move us. Annie Dillard writes that it is the job of the writer not to describe what everyone loves but what only the writer has loved – to bring that tiny bit of the world to the rest of us.

I have been thinking more about the tent caterpillars. Because they are animal, we tend to make an issue of killing them, along with the slugs and the wasps. Why do we think nothing of pulling weeds? Is vegetable consciousness so much less? Or is our consciousness of vegetable consciousness lacking? I think of the title of a May Sarton book, *Plant Dreaming Deep* – such a wonderful image of the crossover of animal/vegetable ways of being. I have begun to think of our assault on the tent caterpillars as a sort of ethnic cleansing. And yet I keep on with my attacks. It is not comfortable and yet we feel justified because they are so ugly and so negligible. I remember how many Buddhists we met in Asia who loved eating meat even though they opposed all killing.

If you move into the woods of southern British Columbia you move into slug country. They were here first. It is less clear with the tent caterpillars. I don't know where they hung out when this country was all Douglas fir. They are creatures parasitic on the plantings of us humans – all the orchard trees, the roses, the berries.

You spoke of the dog wars. We have had years of broom wars. When we bought this farm the upper clearing was solid broom, as high as a car. One year we had a farmer from down the road push the broom into two great heaps up against the firs. That didn't do anything about the broom that lived tucked in the woods, and it was only a temporary solution for the broom in the clearing. It all came back of course. It loves disturbed soil and the backhoe only stimulated its excesses. After that we began to pull it. One spring we invited many friends for a potluck and broom pulling. We began then to get on top of it. Cicely used to hate coming for a walk in the woods with me since it always ended with me pulling broom and her getting fed up.

A biologist friend recently told us about a study that proved that cutting broom is more efficient than pulling it, so this spring I've travelled with clippers. Last week I went on a rampage, cutting the neighbour's broom that grew along the road edge to keep it from seeding into our fields. Everywhere else along the road that offensive metallic yellow of the broom in bloom glares at me, but in our neighbourhood we are almost broom free. Walking in the woods this weekend I was gratified that there were only a few tiny patches of blooming broom, which I could snap off. Not that there aren't lots of little broom plants, but if they are not spreading at least I feel we're holding our own. And the clearing is mostly clear, an open sun-dappled patch that feels like the Promised Land. But it all comes back to that question of who shall live and who shall die. We are all involved in this every day. I keep squashing the tent caterpillars as I mull over these philosophical intricacies. Feeling guilty seems to make me feel better.

I returned from Asia one year and one week ago. We must have started writing these letters shortly after. If we kept on for years would we find the same things to say each fall? Would I remark on the same frozen maple leaves, the same blue of the wild chicory (which is just now sending up its flower stalks)? How cyclical is our consciousness, how much would a new year of letters unfold completely new insights? Today I picked a stalk of wild sorrel. It is flowering, though I only now looked closely enough to see that the small red dots are flowers, not seeds. If it were larger it would be used for dramatic interest in the garden. Since it is so small and not very dramatic, it is a weed. I have foxgloves blooming outside my window, rising up through the cracks in the flagstone. I tried for years to get them to naturalize in the woods and around the farm. For some reason they chose this year to grow in the most inconvenient places. I will not pull them out. It seems too ungrateful.

Walking yesterday I noticed the spikes of fireweed up along the road. Also the grey-green leaves of the pearly everlasting. I remember years ago being impressed when an older friend could identify all sorts of vegetation out the window of a moving car. I could do it now too. It is only a matter of living in one place long enough so that you recognize that this gangly shoot will soon carry graceful rosy pink blossoms and these desiccated lanterns are last year's chocolate lilies. I like learning to recognize the wild plants in all their life stages. It ties the dramatic peak of florescence to the cycle of infancy and senescence.

A soft-hearted friend visited us last week, and as a result, we now have a new kitten found abandoned in a dump with several littermates. He is tiny and stunted, a little ginger male, very outgoing. Maybe finding a place for a stunted one is a way we can care for whatever is stunted within ourselves. Now the bee people just came by to say they are taking the hives tomorrow morning (3 a.m.!) up to the fireweed – a sure sign that summer, in whatever unlikely new form, will actually happen.

Love, Dorothy

p.s. After I wrote this I had a vision of the tent caterpillars talking to me. They were eating away, endlessly eating, and I felt them as an image of the unquenchable life force. They seemed to be saying that no matter how much I squash them I won't make a dent, and that in fact I should take them as a model in their involvement in life, pure life, for its own sake.

A F T E R W O R D

by DOROTHY FIELD

LAST SUMMER WE celebrated our twenty-fifth year on the farm, a full
quarter century. It is still hard for me to believe that creeping time has
flown so. The letters in this book were written in 1995 and 1996. After
that first year of letter writing, Carol and I took a break. In 1997 we
realized how much we both missed the process and began again. Looking through that second year of letters I'm pleased to note that we didn't
just repeat ourselves. There was much that was new to observe and com-
ment on. In Carol's last year, her health deteriorated even further. Physically writing the letters became increasingly difficult. So I am moved to
read a passage she wrote in March, two months before her death: "I can't
bend even to touch things on the ground. I sat in the sun yesterday and
pulled clover from the planter pots on the deck. I marvelled at their
roots full of those nitrogen-fixing nodules. No matter how small my
view of this world, the sights are breathtaking and miraculous." Ron
delivered Carol's last letter to me shortly after she died in May 1998.

I only read Carol's journal excerpts later. It was a painful experience.
There were the events I remembered but now I was seeing them from the
other side of the fence. Apart from Ron, who knew the excruciating
agonies of Carol's illness at first hand, I was among a very few people with
a fairly clear sense of just how hard she struggled. Reading the journals
I learned that there was a depth to the agony I hadn't fully understood,

a leap of imagination I hadn't quite taken. And I don't think that was just chance or my own callousness. Carol held back the grimmest details of her reality. It was as if she couldn't conceive of us "normals" making that leap to understanding, as if she didn't trust our compassion to go that far. And maybe she was right. CFS is still largely uncharted and the unknown holds terror. Being fully with Carol meant being with helplessness, accepting that there wasn't much to offer besides caring and maybe a good story or two from the outside world. It meant suspending the judgments most of us are so quick to make. Being there meant abiding with mystery and human limitation. And it was not always easy to make the space for that receptivity in the whirl and demands of daily life.

Maintaining friendships was a high priority for Carol. Her illness made that difficult – sometimes impossible. Her schedule was rigid. You had to visit during the small windows when she had her greatest energy, confining your time to fifteen or twenty minutes. That made it hard for friends whose schedules didn't match hers or who lived far away. E-mail, her journal and our letters were a godsend. She could compose an e-mail at odd hours when she couldn't sleep, or type in a paragraph or two whenever she had the strength. She fought an ever-increasing isolation as her life became harder and harder for her scattered friends to understand. It was as if she were stranded on a distant planet. Her reality was too foreign and seemingly unbelievable for outsiders to begin to grasp. Reading her journal entries brought back her disappointments over treatments that didn't work, medication that caused horrendous side effects, doctors too stressed or too threatened to connect to the frightened person inside her screaming body. Carol had so much to teach us about living with chronic illness and disability. Unfortunately, the CFS hinged on an exhaustion so deep that she couldn't spare the energy it would have taken to chip away at the medical profession's fear and anxiety in the face of the unknown.

Carol's letters to me were written out of the light — out of the courage and raw interest that kept her engaged with the world. The journals were the nighttime Carol — when there was no face to put on and only an unending series of disappointments. Just as she and Ron came up with a strategy to manage each new downturn (these strategies involved completely reorganizing the house, her schedule, her medication or her exercise plan), the disease would present some new challenge. The journals became the receptacle for the darker thoughts she preferred not to share. Including the journal entries in this book is thus a synthesis and a completion since light is inseparable from shadow. I hope the book in its entirety will widen our understanding of the interplay of richness and constraint that is part of long-term disability.

When I think of Carol I think of a quote from John Cage. He was writing about sound but his words seem appropriate to Carol and the way she lived. "There is no such thing as an empty space or an empty time. There is always something to see, something to hear. In fact, try as we may to make a silence, we cannot. Sounds occur whether intended or not; the psychological turning in the direction of those not intended seems at first to be a giving up of everything that belongs to humanity. But one must see that humanity and nature, not separate, are in this world together, that nothing was lost when everything was given away." (JOHN CAGE, Silence, Wesleyan University Press)

INSECT PASSAGE

for Carol

Wasps in the apples Indian summer –
I wrote about them in a letter to you
how they buzzed the windfalls

bargain hunters at Bay Day.
You wrote of wild bees in their labial hive,
how you sheltered them

till frost dessicated their communion,
and of your garden mutants –
the two-petal trillium (a duallium you called it)

and the accidental squash so huge
you couldn't lift them.
Today hawthorn petals dot sweet rocket.

New kiwi stems nose the air like rosy eels.
Our daily insect passage, seed memories –
Who will I tell now?

—March 1999

A F T E R W O R D

by RON CHUDLEY

CAROL'S GREAT LOVE was gardening, her abiding passion the making of pottery. But one other factor tied these, and all else in her world, together: a compulsion to record. A lifetime of journals set down not only the flow of everyday events but the countless ideas, plans, inventions and wonders that flowed, mostly at breakneck speed, through her endlessly creative mind. Sometimes she would say that to be able to explore all the things she wanted to understand would take at least fifty Carols. So, since there was only one, writing served as a chariot to fly to those many regions that time would not allow her to actually visit.

Little did she know that one day this chariot would become her only means of transport.

Slow but inevitable disease robbed her of everything that took physical strength. Potting went first, then her beloved gardening. In time, even visits from cherished friends and family became too much for her frail body to bear. At last, all that was left was her mind – and the strength to move ten fingers on a keyboard.

For years the computer was not only her recorder and link to the world, it was her lifeline to sanity: the single vital means of expression left by her traitor flesh. With the same abandon which characterized all she did, Carol put the computer to work. An endless stream of letters and e-mails flowed to everyone she knew and loved; a prodigiously detailed

233

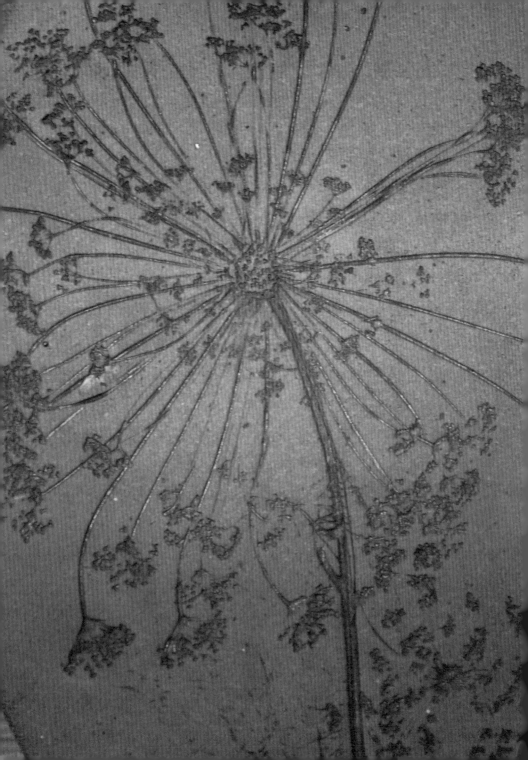

journal documented every moment of our lives. Finally there were the missives which grew to be this book. The creation of *Between Gardens*, shared with her true friend Dorothy, was not only an expression of her irrepressible life force; it turned out to be a high plateau in her dauntless spiritual journey.

Carol and I had only ten years together, but they were the richest in love and sharing of both our lives and their legacy buoys my own heart for whatever span remains. When I think of her now, what my memory lights on most often is her abiding love of nature. In all of this, what really took Carol's breath away were the tantalizingly transient, delicate golds of first spring. It was as if these were a metaphor for her own fragile, all too short existence. "Nothing Gold Can Stay," the poem she mentions in her letters, could well have been about herself.

But the legacy of such gold is summer, a lush season of the heart which lives on in this book — and in the memories of all who knew my wife Carol.

—*March 1999*

C R E D I T S

With thanks to the many gardeners – first and foremost my mother – who brought me into their gardens and opened me to these mysteries.

—DOROTHY FIELD

Text Credits

The quotation from the poem "Nothing Gold Can Stay" (page 34) is from *The Poems of Robert Frost* (New York: Random House, 1930, reissued in 1946), p. 235.

The quotation from the poem "Crazy Jane Talks with the Bishop" (page 108) is from *The Collected Poems of W. B. Yeats* (New York: The Macmillan Company, 1966), p. 254.

The quotation from the Leonard Bernstein musical *Candide* (page 215) is from the song "Make Our Garden Grow," lyrics by Richard Wilbur (Columbia Masterworks Stereo OS 2350).

Image Credits / DOROTHY FIELD

front cover: magnolias (polaroid transfers on handmade paper)
back cover: poppies (polaroid transfer on handmade paper)
interior: pp. 2, 3: lilac (polaroid transfer on handmade paper); p. 6: magnolia (polaroid transfer on handmade paper); p. 11: magnolia (polaroid transfer on handmade paper); p. 15: poppies (polaroid transfer on handmade paper); p. 18: garlic (slide); p. 22: comfrey (polaroid

transfer on handmade paper); pp. 26–27: sunflower (slide); p. 30: eggplant (slide); p. 35: poppies (polaroid transfer on handmade paper); p. 39: squash flower (polaroid transfer on handmade paper); p. 43: quince (slide); p. 50: hollyhock (slide); p. 55: comfrey (polaroid transfer on handmade paper); p. 58: chard (slide); p. 67: Hungarian poppy (slide); pp. 74–75: hops (slide); pp. 78–79: pumpkin (polaroid transfer on handmade paper); p. 82: smoke tree (slide); pp. 86–87: pumpkins (slide); pp. 90–91: maple leaves (slide); pp. 94–95: braken (slide); p. 99: witch hazel (slide); pp. 102–103: peas and beans (slide); p. 106: medlar (slide); pp. 110–111: witch hazel (polaroid transfer on handmade paper); pp. 114–115: hawthorne berries (slide); pp. 118–119: witch hazel (polaroid transfer on handmade paper); pp. 122–123: Korean dogwood (slide); pp. 126–127: raddiccio (slide); p. 130: hazelnut (slide); p. 135: frosty grass (slide); pp. 138–139: *rosa rugosa* (slide); pp. 142–143: witch hazel (slide); p. 147: medlar (slide); pp. 150–151: Japanese green (slide); pp. 154–155: magnolia (polaroid transfer on handmade paper); pp. 158–159: medlar blossoms (polaroid transfer on handmade paper); pp. 162–163: poeny (slide); pp. 170–171: apple blossom (slide); p. 178: maple leaf bud (slide); pp. 186–187: pear blossom (slide); pp. 194–195: sage and santolina (slide); p. 202: hops in April (slide); p. 219: hyacinth (slide); pp. 226–227: lady's mantle (slide); p. 231: pumpkin (polaroid transfer on handmade paper).

Image Credits / CAROL GRAHAM CHUDLEY

Interior: p. 234: detail of pottery (photographed by Dorothy Field); p. 239: detail of pottery (photographed by Dorothy Field)

CAROL GRAHAM CHUDLEY was a gifted potter, teacher and writer. She lived on Vancouver Island, British Columbia, and her home workshop, gallery and gardens were frequented by artists, gardeners and visitors. Despite becoming disabled from the effects of childhood polio and Chronic Fatigue Syndrome, she continued to tend her land and express herself through art until she passed away in the spring of 1998.

DOROTHY FIELD is a writer and papermaker who has lectured and taught courses about handmade paper throughout North America. In addition to *Between Gardens*, she has published a children's book, *In the Street of the Temple Cloth Printers* (Pacific Educational Press), and is a featured poet in *Threshold: Six Women, Six Poets* (edited by Rona Murray, Sono Nis Press). Dorothy Field lives and gardens on a farm on Vancouver Island, British Columbia.

BRIGHT LIGHTS *from* POLESTAR BOOK PUBLISHERS

Polestar Book Publishers takes pride in creating books that enrich our understanding of the world. We support independent voices that illuminate our history, stretch the imagination and engage our sympathies.

NON-FICTION

GARDEN CITY: VANCOUVER
Marg Meikle & Dannie McArthur
1-896095-53-4 · $18.95 · B&W photos and illustrations throughout
Includes lists of nurseries and public gardens, a guide to mail-order seeds, advice on pest-proofing, descriptions of garden clubs, annual events and much, much more. The city-gardener's ultimate resource.

FROM FARM TO FEAST: RECIPES AND STORIES FROM SALTSPRING AND THE SOUTHERN GULF ISLANDS
Gail Richards & Kevin Snook
1-896095-43-7 · $29.95 CDN/$24.95 USA · full-colour photos throughout
Here is the most valuable kind of cookbook: one that renews our relationship with healthy food while revelling in the delights of fine cuisine.

THE GARDEN LETTERS
Elspeth Bradbury & Judy Maddocks
1-896095-06-2 · $19.95 CDN/$15.95 USA · illustrations throughout
"...lively anecdotes and humorous writings about the labours of life and gardening."
— *The Guardian Weekend*

THE REAL GARDEN ROAD TRIP
Elspeth Bradbury & Judy Maddocks
1-896095-35-6 · $24.95 CDN/$19.95 USA · photographs throughout
Longtime friends Elspeth and Judy trek cross-country to find "real gardens and real gardeners."

Polestar titles are available from your local bookseller. For a copy of our catalogue, contact: Polestar Book Publishers, PO BOX 5238, Station B, Victoria, British Columbia Canada V8R 6N4   http://mypage.direct.ca/p/polestar